Power Golf
for Women

Power Golf for Women

How to Hit Longer and Straighter From Tee to Green

Jane Horn

With Illustrations by
Robert Daley

A Citadel Press Book
Published by Carol Publishing Group

A Citadel Press Book
Published by Carol Publishing Group
Citadel Press is a registered trademark of Carol Communications, Inc.

Editorial, sales and distribution, and rights and permissions inquiries should be addressed to Carol Publishing Group, 120 Enterprise Avenue, Secaucus, N.J. 07094.

In Canada: Canadian Manda Group, One Atlantic Avenue, Suite 105, Toronto, Ontario M6K 3E7

Carol Publishing Group books may be purchased in bulk at special discounts for sales promotion, fund-raising, or educational purposes. Special editions can be created to specifications. For details, contact Special Sales Department, Carol Publishing Group, 120 Enterprise Avenue, Secaucus, N.J. 07094.

Manufactured in the United States of America
10   9   8   7   6   5   4   3   2   1

Library of Congress Cataloging-in-Publication Data

Horn, Jane.
    Power golf for women : how to hit longer and straighter from tee
to green / Jane Horn ; with illustrations by Robert Daley.
        p.   cm.
    "A Citadel Press book."
    ISBN 0–8065–2070–1
    1. Golf for women.   2. Swing (Golf)   I. Title.
GV966.H68   1999
796.352′3′082—dc21   99–14069
                                                             CIP

To my mother

for her faith in my abilities

Contents

Introduction:
The Myth of Being Powerless

Changing the Mind-Set

Mind-sets run deep in the golf world. Golf has been traditionally accepted as a man's game, with little room for the avid female golfer. The Victorian notion that a woman has no place in the world of athletics has long been one of golf's favorite tenets. Not only is this not true, but as I have explained in my book *Golf Is a Woman's Game*, women have a greater natural ability for the golf swing than most men. Often mind-sets are self-perpetuating. If it is believed that a woman is incapable of performing a task, then the belief often creates an infrastructure that is designed to impede a woman's success, thus reinforcing the belief. This type of self-perpetuating mind-set can be found in golf instruction.

Golf professionals have assumed that the average female golfer is not capable of hitting the ball any measurable distance. Like any mind-set, the belief makes it a reality. Fortunately, golf is in an era of change; the time is at hand for this belief to be cast aside. Women *can* have a powerful golf game. The problem is that they have been pitted against a formidable bias that has labeled them as players without power.

Golf instructors have been the most prominent perpetrators of this power myth, teaching that it is easier to accept than to change. Many a golf professional's attitude when teaching a woman is "What's the use? She's never going to be able to get any distance." Once this attitude is adopted, there is very little hope for a woman to improve the distance in her game.

However, golf is not a game of muscle; it is a game of technique. I have seen women with medium builds and average strength hit the ball farther than anyone had imagined because they employed the proper swing techniques. Both women and men, despite their strength, can hit the ball far enough to enjoy the game. However, before this can be done, one must learn the proper sources of power and dispel certain misconceptions about the golf swing.

This book is designed for beginning-to-advanced golfers who truly want to hit the ball farther. Most women do not realize that with the proper swing concepts the extra 10 yards they desire can be a reality. *Power Golf for Women* will supply you with concepts and drills that, if followed correctly, will easily add the yardage you so desperately desire. Because the majority of golfer's are right-handed, the instruction in this book was written for the right-handed golfer. If you are left-handed please do not be deterred, the theory and instruction are the same only reversed.

Before you proceed to the following chapters, clear your mind. Forget all the lessons and what you have been told you can or cannot accomplish. Read this book not as a woman with preconceived limitations but as a human being who loves and enjoys the game of golf and wants to hit the ball farther. Once this is done, you will be free to absorb all the information that will enable you to acquire the distance you need.

PART I

The Anatomy of a Powerful Swing

1

Power Factors

As I explained in my book *Golf Is a Woman's Game*, power in a golf swing does not result from conventional methods. For example, when swinging a golf club, one's natural inclination would be to deliver the club head directly back to the ball, with all the force possible. In other sports this may work well, but in golf it does not. There are four factors which determine distance and accuracy in the golf swing.

The first power factor is club-head speed. Club-head speed can be a very confusing concept. Most golfers will instinctively use the wrong part of their anatomy in an attempt to generate speed, most commonly the forearms and hands, assuming that at impact the snapping of the hands and wrists generates club-head speed. This common misconception, however, often leads to a loss of power. When you try to force the club head to move faster, you actually lose speed at the moment of impact.

Club-head speed is created by club-head lag; that is, the club head lagging behind the hands on the downswing (see Fig. 1). Using your wrists to force the club head at the ball is called "throwing the club," or "casting the club," which results in a loss of lag pressure. Your lag pressure will increase when the club head stays behind the hands on the downswing. Ideally, the

FIGURE 1. The club head lags behind the hands on the downswing.

weight of the club head will catch up to the swinging hands by gravitational and inertial effects. If this happens correctly, the hands will lead on the downswing, and at impact the hands will be slightly ahead of the club face, with the left wrist slightly pronated. This is the pinnacle of power in the golf swing (see Fig. 2). If, at any point on your downswing, the club head happens to get ahead of the hands in meeting the ball, you are not swinging optimally. Your optimum point of speed would have been reached if the club head had caught up with—not passed—the swinging arms and hands. Not only are you losing acceleration when the club head passes the hands; other power factors, such as the direction in which the club head is pointing and the path that it is on at impact, are virtually out of control. You will notice that with the hands leading (see Fig. 2), the club face is pointing toward your target while it is traveling on the correct path.

The second power factor is the part of the club head that meets the ball. There are three parts to the club face: the closest to the shaft, the heel; the center; and the toe. Hitting a ball on one of these different areas can add or detract from your distance. Ideally, we would like to hit the ball on the club's sweet spot. Every club

FIGURE 2. The hands lead the club head at impact.

FIGURE 3A. When the club takes a downswing path that comes across the ball, left of the target line, it has taken an outside-to-inside downswing path.

has a sweet spot, and usually this is located at the club face's center. This sweet spot makes maximum use of club-head speed. Usually this area has been optimized by the manufacturer's use of proper weighting and distribution of mass. When hit, the ball will spring off the sweet spot almost effortlessly. Conversely, a shot hit off the club's heel or toe may result in a powerless shot. A tee shot hit off either the heel or toe could cost up to 15 yards. Thus, one can see that the area that strikes the ball is going to be quite important.

The third power factor is the direction the club face is pointing at impact. You want the ball to meet the sweet spot, but if at impact the club face is pointed in the wrong direction, this is not going to happen. A ball hit with all the force in the world won't help your game if it travels dead left or right because the ball struck the wrong part of the club face.

The club's swing path, or the direction and angle at which the swinging club approaches the ball, is the fourth power factor. The swing path can have control over all the other factors, so it is usually the most discussed and corrected part of the swing.

The downswing can take one of three different paths: outside to inside, square to square, or inside to outside (see Figs. 3A, B, and C). As you can see from the illustrations, one obvious effect of the swing path is the direction the ball travels. You can also see

FIGURE 3B. When the club arrives squarely to the ball, pointing toward the target, it has taken a square downswing path.

FIGURE 3C. When the club face approaches the ball from the left of the target line and then swings out to the right, it has taken an inside-to-outside downswing path.

how it will affect the part of the club face that will make contact with the ball and what direction the club face will be pointing at impact. These factors will not only affect the type of spin imparted to the ball but also, most importantly, club-head lag.

Let me give you an example of the effect of the swing path. Most golfers have an outside-to-inside downswing path, commonly called "coming over the ball." Many falsely believe that any degree of coming over or across the ball on the downswing is bad. However, the consequences of such a swing path depend largely on its severity. For your average golfer, the severity is usually considerable. If the club comes from outside to inside and at the moment of impact your club face is pointing toward your target, you will create a slice—a shot that starts straight and then veers sharply toward the right (also often called a banana ball). Not only does a slice produce an inaccurate shot, it also loses power. The average sliced drive easily measures 15–20 yards shorter than normal.

The angle at which the club descends onto the ball is also affected by this swing path. An outside-to-inside path will create a steeper angle of descent and will affect the type of blow imparted to the ball and club-head lag. When a steep, descending blow is imparted on a tee shot, the momentum and force of the club travel downward, not toward the target. Consequently, much energy and momentum are lost. This downward direction will also produce a backspin on the ball, resulting in a higher-than-normal trajectory. Another important consideration is the loss of club-head lag. When you create a steep descending plane, it becomes harder for the wrists to maintain their 90-degree angle. This, in turn, creates a casting motion, which results in decreased lag pressure. Once this occurs, the club head becomes out of control, and literally any shot can result. Most importantly, this casting motion translates into a loss of power. One can see how something as simple as the downswing path can have major consequences on creating power.

As you read this book, keep these four power factors in mind. Every movement discussed in the following chapters will affect at least one or more of these closely related power factors.

The Power Angle and Lag Pressure

The 90-degree wrist cock formed during the backswing will be referred to here as the power angle. The importance of this angle is that it creates club-head lag. Remember that our natural inclination is to deliver the club head directly back to the ball. In golf this is not desired. Ideally, we want the club head to lag behind the swinging hands, building up club-head lag pressure (see Fig. 4). Experiment for yourself. Hold the club in your left hand. Now swing the club back without cocking your wrist and follow through. Notice that the club head can travel at a speed no faster than the swinging arm, so the arm speed would be almost equal to the club-head speed. Now cock your wrist on the backswing and follow through. You will now see that the 90-degree wrist hinge—the power angle—has given the club the ability to swing much faster than the arms. Since the club head follows a succession of downswing movements, you are creating a whiplike effect whose speed is optimized in the hitting zone. Every movement or position that we create, from the address to the downswing, is a movement that will facilitate the maintenance of the power angle and create lag pressure.

FIGURE 4. The power angle, which is the 90-degree wrist cock, creates power on the downwing.

POWER TIP

One of the biggest problems for women is the loss of the power angle. Often, in an attempt to hit the ball harder, many women try to force the club head at the ball (commonly called club-head throwaway or casting; see Fig. 5). This will not give you the consistent distance you need. Power is technique, not muscle, and when you learn the proper technique, you will hit the ball farther with half the effort.

FIGURE 5. The straightening of the power angle during the downswing is called casting, or club-head throwaway.

FIGURE 6. Rear view of the power assembly.

Your Power Assembly

Your power assembly is a power source created by the position of your wrists, arms, and shoulders at the top of the backswing (see Fig. 6). It not only includes the power angle; it will facilitate its movement on the downswing. To create the power assembly, your shoulders must be turned and your wrists cocked 90 degrees. Your hands should be extended from your body, with the left arm straight or slightly bowed. The right arm should be bent in a supportive position (not cocked). Once in position, this assembly will move together on the downswing. The assembly's unified movement is crucial to keeping the power angle on the downswing.

POWER TIP

The power assembly will look different, depending on the length of your arms, the restriction of your shoulder turn, and your backswing plane (see chapter 4). Short arms, a restricted shoulder turn, and a flat backswing all force the right elbow to be positioned close to the body at the top of the backswing.

The Left Arm in the Power Assembly

The left arm should be straight but not because of tension and should not be broken (cocked at the elbow). The left arm will remain straight for several reasons. First, because the club was gripped properly at the address, and second, because the arms will maintain the same distance from the body as at the address. If your left elbow bows slightly at the top of your swing, do not worry too much; this is acceptable. However, your left arm should not break at the top of your swing. When the left arm breaks on the downswing, the straightening of the left arm will force the wrists to lose their power angle and lag pressure. Conversely, a stiff left arm will make it hard for the wrists to hinge and thus form the power angle.

The Right Arm in the Power Assembly

The right-arm position is rarely discussed but is a very important aspect of the power assembly. In the correct position, the right arm creates a vicelike position that is supportive of the club and the left arm. Once locked in this position, this arm enables the power assembly to stay together on the downswing (see Fig. 7).

FIGURE 7. The outward pressure from the right arm keeps the left arm extended. The right arm remains in this position at the start of the downswing.

Ideally, on the backswing, the right elbow bends in deference to the cocking wrists. If, instead of bending, the elbow itself cocks, the right arm will be placed in a far too powerful position. As such, the first move on the downswing will more than likely be the uncocking of the elbow, which will create a casting motion (see Fig. 8).

The Power Center

Place your left hand on your chest just below your collarbone. This is your power center. The power center is the golf swing's motor (see Fig. 9). In a correct swing, the speed of the center's downswing rotation should be directly correlated to the club head's speed. Theoretically, the faster and more powerful the center's movement, the more speed transmitted to the club head. This center will rotate 90 degrees to the right on the backswing and return 180 degrees to the left on the downswing.

FIGURE 8. A cocked right elbow will force a casting motion on the downswing

FIGURE 9. The power center's 90-degree rotation on the backswing.

POWER TIP
The fact that your downswing appears to be "all arms" is usually an indication that your power center is not making a full backswing rotation. Be sure that on your backswing your shoulders are making a 90-degree turn.

Power Anchors

Parts of the body, which, by their anchoring effect, create more torque or rotational speed are called power anchors. In the golf swing, the hips act as primary power anchors. The torque created by their 45-degree angle and the shoulder's 90-degree turn will enable the power center to move at a faster rate. (You will learn more about power anchors in later chapters.)

Timing and Power

Timing in a golf swing is somewhat analogous to pistons firing in an engine. It is a chain of separate events that, when put together, forms a smooth, cohesive action. In the golf swing, timing refers to the body's movement in relation to the swinging club. When a golfer's timing is on, the body swings the club in the most efficient and productive manner possible. When a golfer's timing is off, the body feels as if it is out of whack, and more energy is creating less output. It takes very little to throw off the timing of a golf swing. Something as simple as the hips moving a little too quickly on the downswing can disrupt the sequence of events, which results in a mis-hit shot. Conversely, timing can make a swing with many faults produce a good shot.

We now have discussed the four power factors and the parts of the anatomy that will be primarily responsible for the production of power. We have also seen how timing will act as the cohesive agent that will be essential if maximum power is to be achieved. In the following chapters we will put together the pieces that will create the *power swing*.

2

The Power Grip

To grip the club, hold your left hand at a 45-degree tilt, with the fingers pointing toward the ground. With the right hand, place the club's handle diagonally across the fingers of the left hand's first joint. Now place the heel of the left hand on top of the club's shaft and grip with all your fingers (see Figs. 10 and 11). You will want to make sure that the thumb of the left hand is pointing toward the right side of the club's shaft. The thumb and index finger of the left hand should create a *V*. The left hand should be placed about a quarter inch from the club's butt. With the right hand, as with the left hand, tilt the fingers at a 45-degree angle, pointing toward the ground.

FIGURE 11. The position of left hand on the club.

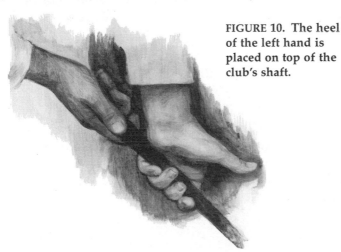

FIGURE 10. The heel of the left hand is placed on top of the club's shaft.

FIGURES 12A and B. The club is laid between the first and second knuckles of the right hand.

FIGURE 13. The grip.

Now grip the club so that it lies in the first joint of the right hand (see Figs. 12A and 12B). Close your hand so that the thumb of the right hand points down the left side of the club's shaft and the thumb of the left hand fits into the palm of the right hand (see Fig. 13). You have three options as to the placement of the right hand's little finger. In the overlapping grip, the little finger is positioned between the index and middle fingers of the left hand. With the interlocking grip the little finger is intertwined with the index finger of the left hand. In the baseball, or natural, grip, the little finger wraps around the club's shaft and rests next to the index finger of the left hand (see Figs. 14A, B, and C).

Use whichever grip feels right for you. However, I would not suggest using the baseball grip unless you have very small, weak hands. Ideally, both hands should work together. If you are right-handed, there will be a tendency for your right hand to dominate in this situation. The other two grips weaken the right hand by removing the pressure from the little finger. Choose the grip that is most comfortable for you. If no one grip particularly suits you, then use the one that is easiest to remember.

Pressure Points for Power

A grip should be defined as the hand's position and its pressure points. When teaching the grip, many golf professionals place the golfer's hands on the club in the correct position and neglect to mention the proper pressure points. There is a big difference between positioning the hands and gripping the club. And this difference translates into more power in the golf swing. A correct grip ensures that the proper pressure is applied. This correct application of pressure employs different muscles in the hands and the forearms. Not only do these muscles affect the club's position on the backswing; they also have a direct relationship to the amount of clubhead speed you generate on the downswing.

I think it was Ben Hogan who stated that the swing is all in the grip, and I couldn't agree with him more. Take a club and experiment. First, grip the club in the palms of your hands. Notice that this tenses the hands and the forearms and shoulders. Now grip the club more toward your fingers. You should feel less tension in the arms and shoulders. This time, when you grip the club, apply pressure with different

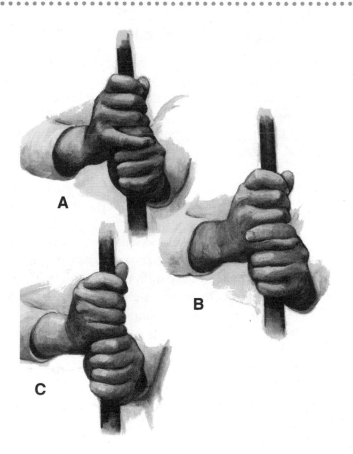

FIGURE 14. A, the
overlapping grip;
B, the interlocking grip;
C, the baseball grip.

fingers and areas of the hand. Notice what is happening in your arms—various muscles and tendons in the arm tighten because of your hand's pressure. This tension has a direct impact on your backswing. An incorrect pressure point can cause tension in a muscle that could have a variety of consequences. For example, the wrists may not hinge correctly, or perhaps the club's backswing path may be affected. In any case, an altered backswing will affect the downswing, which usually means a loss of power.

Everyone's hand has a different conformation. Consequently, to grip the club correctly, your hand position may differ from another's. Different-sized grips can accommodate different hand sizes, but this does not compensate for all the individual differences. Let's say your fingers are very long and the width of your hand is narrow. You'll want to make the width of your hand play a stronger or more dominant role by gripping the club more toward the fingers, enabling the left hand's heel to get on top of the club's shaft. The only way to know how to grip the club correctly is to know exactly what you want the grip to accomplish.

The Power Grip on the Backswing

POWER TIP

When you grip the club with your right hand, first squeeze the club in your fingers and allow your thumb's heel pad (the fleshy part of the palm at the thumb's base) to gently cover your left thumb. Too much pressure exerted by your thumb's heel pad will put tension in the right arm and force the club to take an outside backswing path.

The first function of the grip is to ensure the correct club placement at the top of the backswing. To do this, the wrists must be able to hinge correctly, and the arms should be relatively tension free. Position the handle so that it lies at the point where the fingers meet the hand (see Fig. 15). When you close your fingers, make sure that pressure is applied with the last three fingers of the left hand and the middle two fingers of the right hand. Your thumbs should be placed off to the opposite sides. In other words, the thumb of the right hand should point to the left side, and the thumb of the left hand should point to the right. The reason for this is simple. On the backswing your wrists will cock 90 degrees. The thumbs applying pressure directly down the shaft of the club will make it very difficult for the wrists to make their full 90-degree cock. To ensure a correct wrist cock, the flat part of the left thumb pad and the right half of the right thumb pad should be exerting very light pressure against the sides of the shaft.

At the top of your backswing, the back of your left hand should be slightly concave. This will happen naturally if the hands are placed on the club correctly. However, if you happen to grip the club too tightly in the palm of your hands, you will find that at the top of your backswing the back of the left hand will be flat, putting your club head in an incorrect position.

When gripping the club with the left hand, it is extremely important to place the heel of the left hand on top of the club's shaft (see Figs. 16A and B). When gripping correctly, you should feel your left arm straighten at the address. This straightening does not come from tension. When your left hand's heel is on top of the club's shaft, the left arm becomes slightly contorted and actually straightens. This helps provide the firmness the left arm needs to dominate the backswing. It also facilitates the correct motion for the wrist cock.

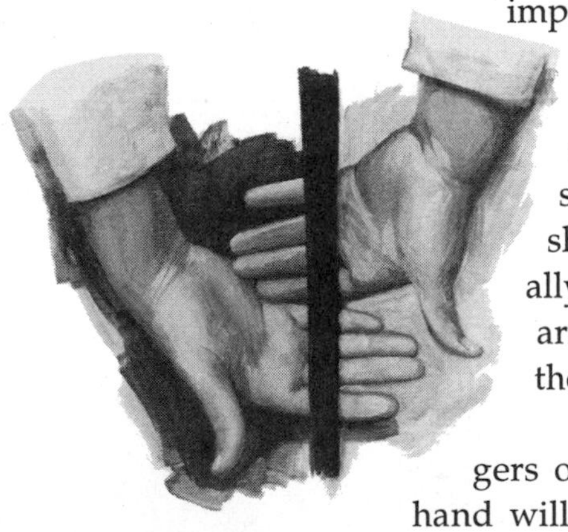

It is equally important to position the club in the fingers of the right hand. If you are right-handed, the right hand will tend to dominate the backswing. One way we can fight this tendency is to weaken the right hand's strength on the club at the address. This can be accomplished by placing the club in the fingers. The right hand's index finger creates a talonlike position (see Figs. 12A and B), while the thumb gently squeezes

FIGURE 15. The club's shaft should lay between the fingers' first and second joints.

FIGURE 16A. The heel of the left hand on top of the club.

FIGURE 16B. When you apply pressure with the last two fingers and the heel of the left hand the wrists will naturally cock.

POWER TIP

If you have petite hands you probably don't have much width between your left hand's thumb and its heel. In this case it is important to have the heel on top of the shaft. Otherwise, the club will slip into your palm.

POWER TIP

If you feel you are holding the club too tightly, it could be that the club is situated too far into the palm of your hand. Holding the club in the palm of one's hand requires pressure from the entire hand, which produces tension in the forearms. If you situate the club more toward the fingers, they can hold it firmly and apply half the tension required by the palms.

the left side of the club's shaft. The little finger of the right hand should either overlap or intertwine with the index finger of the left hand. Removing the little finger of the right hand from the club's shaft weakens the right hand, ensuring that the hands work as a unit. Most golfers have a tendency to put the club in the palm of their right hand. This placement will lead to some serious problems in the backswing. The club face will usually wind up in a closed position at the top of the swing. Moreover, there will be a tendency for the right hand to snatch the club at take-away rather than letting the left hand dominate. Another possible problem is that this grip could lead to a roundhouse backswing. (The club moves horizontally around the body rather than vertically into position.) Thus, the placement of the club in the right hand's palm will cause nothing but trouble on the back-swing. An equally troublesome position is achieved by placing the club too far into the fingers of the right hand. This forces the right arm out of its relaxed position and makes it straighter— and more dominant. This position will push the club outside its normal swing path on the backswing and create problems on the downswing.

The Power Grip at the Top of the Backswing

At the top of the backswing the hand position remains the same as at the address; only the pressure points will vary. For the right hand, the index finger should be as at the address, positioned in a talonlike manner (see Fig. 17). The shaft of the club will be supported by the first joint of the index finger, with very slight side pressure from the right side of the thumb, which will nestle the club into the talon grip. Positioned in the fingers, the club's shaft

FIGURE 17. The club's shaft is nestled in the right hand's index finger.

POWER TIP
If you are right-handed, it is perfectly normal for your right hand to dominate on the downswing. Be sure you use the same pressure points for the right hand on the downswing as you used on the backswing—the middle two fingers of the right hand. During the downswing, it is common for these points to shift to the thumb and index finger, which will create a casting motion.

will rest on the pads. Where the fingers meet, the hand and the club will be supported by a slightly upward pressure from the palm of the right hand.

In the left hand the club will be lightly supported by the thumb, with pressure from the last three fingers of the left hand. The heel of the left hand should provide pressure upward, which will support the club by locking the shaft into a viselike position.

The Power Grip on the Downswing

If your club position and wrist cock are correct, you should be ready to execute the downswing. The top of your backswing will reflect your grip position at the address. If, at the address, you have gripped the club so that the heel of the left hand is on top of the club's shaft, you will have created a viselike effect. This effect will be important in maintaining the power angle (see chapter 1) on the downswing (see chapter 6). The pressure exerted by the heel of the left hand should enable you to maintain this angle longer on the downswing. Also, it is important that the thumb pressure on the club's shaft be light and on the sides of the handle. The thumbs pointing directly down the club's shaft during the downswing will straighten the angle created by the wrists. Another grip factor that can cause an early release in the downswing is gripping the club in the palms rather than the fingers. Without the heel of the left hand on top of the club, the palms will have a difficult time maintaining the power angle, resulting in a casting motion (club-head throwaway).

By experimenting and applying these different pressure points, you should see a gradual improvement in your distance. So many people take the grip for granted, but without a proper grip, it is almost impossible to get the distance you require. It is imperative that you associate technique and positioning, not physical force, with power. If you practice these pressure points, you will witness rapid improvement (see chapter 6 to learn more about downswing-grip pressure points).

Constructive Versus Destructive Tension

There are two different types of tension in a golf swing: constructive and destructive. Constructive tension means that your body is flexed, ready to anticipate and react. Destructive tension creates a type of paralysis. You are no longer prepared to make an athletic motion. Rather, your body has placed itself in a control mode in which every move becomes part of a mental process, not a natural reaction. The old saying "Analysis leads to paralysis" could not be more true than in the game of golf.

Ideally, we want to advance our swing from the beginning level of a contrived motion, where each part of the swing is thought out individually, to the advanced level of reactive motion, when you sense the correct reaction to the stimulus of the golf ball and target. In this process, tension will have a great deal of influence. One major source of tension lies in the grip.

POWER TIP
To produce maximum power, the palm of the right hand should be pointing down the target line at impact. A good grip at the address increases the probability of this occurring.

The "Death Grip"

Many players grip the club with what I call a "death grip." This is when the golfer grips the club as if she is hanging on for dear life! The problem is, when you use a death grip, you are tensing muscles not only in your hands but in your forearms and shoulders as well. This tension (as we have seen) will affect both your backswing and downswing. When you have hand and arm tension, the result is stiffness in the wrists and the inability to create a 90-degree power angle. For this reason, beginning players have problems with cocking the wrists and bending the left elbow on the backswing. When the left elbow chronically bends, it is because the wrists cannot. Mentally you have a picture of where the club should be placed (parallel to the ground). If the wrists are unable to put the club into this position (because of tension), the arms will intervene and function as the wrists. So instead of the wrists, the elbows will cock (see Fig. 8).

There is really nothing you can do to stop beginners from having a death grip. They need to learn to feel confident that, when swinging, the club will not fly out of their hands. One way to promote such security is to teach the beginner to swing the club with one hand. If the golfer is right-handed, I will often start with the right arm; it should be stronger and therefore easier for the newcomer to control. Once she is secure with the right hand, then it is time to try with the left. After more than a dozen swings with each arm, both hands are placed on the grip. After just a few swings, the tension will subside as the golfer learns that it is possible to hold on to the club with just one hand. Thus, "two hands should be easy!"

POWER TIP

At the address, do not grip the club while it is touching the ground. Instead, hold the club so that it points toward the sky and then place your hands correctly on the shaft. This accomplishes two tasks. First, it keeps you from creating tension by pressing the club head into the ground. Second, when you grip the club in the air, you have a better feel for the weight of the club and the proper pressure points.

POWER TIP

After several practice swings, make sure that you regrip your club or just open your hands to release the pressure. On the follow-through, the pressure exerted by the hands just to hold on to the club increases tenfold. Consequently, on the golf course, after two practice swings without releasing the grip pressure, your muscles will be far too tense to execute the golf swing correctly.

Intermediate-to-advanced golfers who apply a death grip will find that the same exercise with a slightly different twist will be effective. First, execute six swings with your right arm and then with your left. Now take six more swings with the right arm; only this time grip the club with your right hand, holding it with just your fingers. Now swing the club back and forth. Once you realize you can hold on to the club with just your fingers, when you assume your normal grip, your grip pressure will automatically be more relaxed. Also, try this exercise with the left hand. Only this time grip with the index finger of the left hand, nestling the butt of the club under the heel of your left hand. Again, swing back and forth with just one finger and the heel of the left hand on the club.

A major source of destructive tension exists not only at the address but also while the club is in motion. Ideally, we want the same grip pressure at the address as on the backswing and downswing. However, there is an instinctive need to grip the club tighter when you begin to swing. If you were chopping wood, you would feel your hands tense on the ax handle as you chopped down. This is normal, because to hit into a solid object and maintain your grip you need to increase hand pressure. When you swing back toward a golf ball, the same type of response is elicited. The hands will naturally increase in pressure preparing to hit a solid object, namely, the ball. But this increase in pressure has to be kept to a minimum. If the pressure is going to dramatically increase, at least let it do so at the correct pressure points. This increase in tension on the downswing can promote club-head throwaway or casting (see chapter 6).

The instinctual need to increase grip pressure on the downswing is overridden by seasoned professionals. The more advanced the golfer, the more balanced her grip pressure will be throughout her swing. Men, who have strong hands and forearms, tend to increase grip pressure in the swing more dramatically. This detracts from the technique employed in their swing (the premise of my first book, *Golf Is a Woman's Game*) and contributes to pure brute force.

Confidence is also a contributing factor in equalizing grip pressure during your swing. The more confident you are in your swing, the more likely you are to hit the ball well. That is why many golfers say that their swing felt great on a day when they had an excellent round of golf. Their muscles were relaxed, and their swing employed technique rather than brute force.

Proper Grip Size

Another way to accommodate differences in hand size is to use an appropriately sized grip. Manufactured in men's and ladies' sizes, grips can be customized, either oversized or undersized, based on the structure of your hands. Many women have problems gripping the club properly because their grip size is incorrect. You could have the most expensive, up-to-date golf clubs; however, without being gripped correctly, they are not worth their weight in salt. If you are having difficultly keeping the club positioned in your fingers, your grips are probably too large. Conversely, if your hand just seems to wrap around the club, your grips are too small. So remember, grips are not like gloves, where one size fits all. They should be customized and are as important as the quality of the club that you are using.

POWER TIP

Be sure to check your grips periodically for wear. A rubber grip that is worn will become hard and slippery. Since this process does not happen overnight, you might not even notice the wear. However, often without your even being aware, the grip's slipperiness will cause your grip pressure to increase. The cost of a new set of grips is well worth preventing the potential damage that too much grip pressure can have on your swing.

3

The Power Stance

Many golfers do not realize the importance of a proper stance in creating power. Not only will the stance dictate power factors, such as swing path and club-face direction, it will also poise your body in an angled position that will ensure maximum acceleration at impact.

When addressing the ball, your first step will be to slightly flex your knees and bend from your hips about 45 degrees. Your feet should be completely together with the ball in the center of your stance. Hold the club with your left hand so that the club head is directly behind the ball and pointing toward your target. Your left arm should hang vertically, with the left hand an extended hand's length away from your body (see Figs. 18 and 19). Now spread your feet about a shoulder's length apart so that the ball is positioned slightly left of the center. You can now grip the club with your right hand. Your arms and the shaft of the club should form the letter Y, and your shoulders, hips, and feet should all be in parallel alignment.

This is the traditional manner in which you address a ball. Let me now explain how this address position will affect power in your swing.

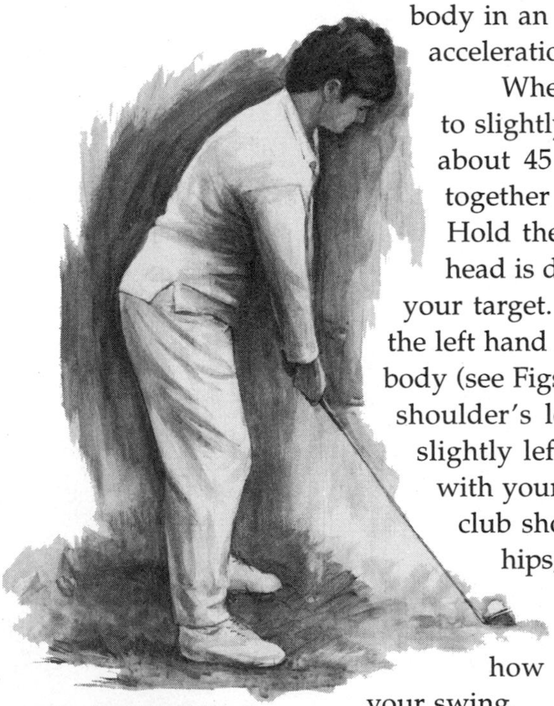

FIGURE 18. Side view of the stance.

Power Anchors

Hips

One of the most important things you can do to create a powerful stance is to secure your power anchors. For most women, the hips are the primary power anchors; they create a lower center of gravity, which stabilizes and anchors the golf swing. In acting as an anchor, they will also create torque between the upper and lower body on the backswing. Traditionally, women have been taught to bend from the waist, which detracts from using the hips as an anchor. To be used effectively, we must assume an address position that will complement the hips' role as an anchor.

At the address, make a 45-degree bend from your hip joint. (You should feel that holding a heavy object would be no problem; however, if you were to bend any further, you could not do so.) When you bend at the hips, your spine should feel fairly straight. Do not try to make it straight by being stiff. The mere bending at the hip joint should permit this to happen naturally. Make sure that when you bend from your hips you only bend slightly at the neck. In other words do not try to look directly at the ball; rather, peer down toward the ball. This posture should be maintained until after the ball is hit.

Many of you have felt your body pull up and away from the ball on the downswing. This is called "coming out of your posture." Bending correctly at the address increases the probability that your posture will be maintained. When bending, target the two hip joints. Feel as if there is a metal rod extending from the left hip to the right hip joint and that this rod segments the upper body from the lower body. This rod is the axle on which you should bend. The role of this position will be addressed further in the chapters on the backswing and downswing.

Legs and Feet

When you address the ball, think of your legs and feet in a tripod position with the feet about shoulder width apart and toes pointed slightly outward (penguin style). As with any athletic feat, your knees should be slightly flexed. You must remember that your lower body is a base on which the upper body turns. It is very important that this base provides stability and is not rigid.

POWER TIP

The distance between your feet in your stance supplies more than balance. It tells your mind how much motion is necessary. With a narrow stance, your brain will expect very little motion. A wider stance implies more motion and the need for balance. The backswing is for position, not a windup (see chapter 4). This is why it is important to keep your stance about shoulder width—just enough to supply balance and send the message to the brain that you are swinging into a position.

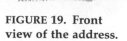

FIGURE 19. Front view of the address.

Shoulders

The third anchor, the shoulders, can affect the upper body by putting your power center into motion. For this reason, they should be set up to turn as smoothly and evenly as possible. When you address the ball and after you have taken care of the other two power anchors, think about your shoulder caps. You should feel your arms hanging vertically from the caps so that your hands are about an extended-hand's length away from your body. Once you are set to your target, you should pump your forearms back and forth to rid your arms of any unnecessary tension.

When you view the shoulders' address position, you may notice that the right shoulder is slightly lower than the left. Do not intentionally lower this shoulder. The tilt of this shoulder depends on the length of your right arm and your grip position. That the right-hand grip is lower on the shaft will naturally lower the right shoulder. However, if your right arm is longer than your left, the tilt will be to a lesser degree. A grip in which the club lies too much in the palm of the right hand will also force the right shoulder down.

The length of the right arm will determine the flex at its elbow. We have seen how the arms should hang straight, from gravity, not from tension. However, if the right arm is longer than the left, its elbow will have a slight bend.

These anchors are all crucial for the execution of a proper golf swing and very easy to practice. I cannot emphasize enough how good posture (bending properly from the hip) at the address can enable you to increase your distance off the tee. In setting these power anchors, we must first be sure that they are aligned properly.

Aligning Your Body for Power

Correct alignment is very important in a power swing. The power factor most affected by incorrect alignment is the club's backswing path. In chapter 1 we discussed how the swing path determines not only the direction the ball will travel but also the part of the club face that contacts the ball. It is therefore important that your body is aligned correctly at the beginning to help produce a correct backswing.

When addressing the ball, your shoulders, hips, and feet should be in parallel alignment, with the club face pointing toward your target. Many golfers approach the ball trying to align their feet or shoulders to the target. Your feet and shoulders should not be used for alignment; rather, they should be positioned in respect to your target line. When setting up to your target, first make sure that your club head is pointing toward your target; then align your shoulders, hips, and feet parallel with this target line. This will determine a swing path that will complement the club's alignment.

In golf there are three different positions relative to the target line that the body or the club face can assume: open, square, and closed. Open (regarding your body) is when any or all of your power anchors are not parallel but instead create an angle with your target line that points to the left. In a square position, all anchors are parallel to the target line. In a closed position, the anchor's angle will point to the right. If your power anchors are not aligned correctly at the address, the chances of your hitting the ball with any force are diminished.

The Tendency to Align to the Right of the Target

We have all played golf with someone who aims too far right of their target. So much so that one wonders how the heck they even hit the ball! It is even more amazing when they manage to hit the ball toward their target! However, this is often not the case. Instead, the ball ends up going where they have aimed, dead right, or in a subconscious attempt to hit the ball toward their target, they end up pulling it dead left. Most golfers have probably tried to tell, or have been told by, someone else that they were aimed too far right of their target. The following dialogue occurs every day on the golf course and may sound familiar to you. You tell your friend, "You're pointed too far toward the right." To which she replies, "No, I'm not. I'm aimed right over there," and she points toward the target with the club's shaft over her left shoulder. You retort, "You're aimed right toward those trees; that's why the ball went into the woods." "Are you sure?" she asks, astonished. You reply, "Look," and then lay a club on the ground that touches the tips of her shoes. As she steps back to see where the club is pointing, she utters, "Oh, my, I'm pointed right into the woods!" After gleefully proving your point, you set up to hit your tee shot, not realizing that you are also pointed far right of your destination. Aiming right is a common malady among women. Let me explain why.

The tendency to aim to the right usually goes hand in hand

At the address, you want your arms to hang straight from the shoulder caps, as if you were going to perform a dive into a pool.

with the desire for more distance. Aiming toward the right is your body's natural way to produce power. When the body is aimed toward the right, it creates greater leverage for the swinging arms. This works well if you are chopping wood, but in the golf swing it does not always have a powerful effect. You have to retrain your subconscious to understand that playing golf is different from chopping wood. Aiming to the right on occasion will make the ball travel farther; however, for your basic swing, it is not desired. Ideally, we want all our power anchors to be in parallel alignment, creating a correct backswing path, which will hopefully lead to a power position on the downswing.

Picking an Intermediary Target

One method of alignment that can be helpful is to pick an intermediate target. This means picking a target that is in a straight line with your original target, only closer. First, stand directly behind your ball, in a straight line with the ball and the target. Visualize a line extending from the ball to the target. Next, pick a spot that is on your imaginary target line, only closer to the ball. This spot can be a leaf, a patch of discolored grass, or any object. Now, when you address the ball, be sure that the club face is pointing toward this object and then align your body so that it is parallel to the club face. Theoretically, if you are aligned toward a target that is on a straight line with your original target, you will also be aligned toward the original target. This is what is meant by an intermediary target; this method can be very helpful to anyone who has chronic problems with alignment—and a low supply of golf balls!

The Ball Position in the Power Stance

When using an iron, the ball should be played slightly left of the stance's center for the beginner-to-intermediate golfer. With the woods, the ball should be in straight alignment with the left heel. Ideally, with different clubs, the bottom of the arc should be the same. You will notice that with the shorter clubs you stand closer to the ball at the address; with the longer clubs, you stand farther away. The theory behind this is that the same relative distance must be maintained with the different-length clubs. The body's position is adjusted to accommodate the difference in lengths between clubs. The same holds true for the ball's position in relation to the feet. With various-length clubs, the bottom of the swing's arc will be slightly different. As the club increases in length, the bottom of its arc will move left of the stance's center. With an iron, the ball should be struck at the bottom of the swing's arc. With the woods, the ball should be struck on the upswing. This is why the wood should be played with the ball positioned in alignment with the left heel and the iron slightly left of the center.

Some believe that the shortest iron (the pitching wedge) should be played in the middle of your stance. With the increase in the shaft's length, the ball should be played progressively left of your center until you reach the driver, in which case the ball should be positioned in straight alignment with the left heel. I believe that all irons should be played in the same position, with the three-iron positioned slightly more toward the left heel than the other irons, for several reasons. Loss of power in a golf swing is usually caused by club-head throwaway, or casting. When a ball is played too far back in the stance (toward the right foot), there is a tendency to want to cast the club head. However, if the ball is positioned slightly left of the stance's center, it is easier to maintain your power angle longer. This position will create greater lag pressure and consequently more club-head speed. Moreover, it is just plain confusing for beginning-to-intermediate golfers to have to modify the ball's position every time they put a different iron into their hand, and the scientific basis for such modification has always seemed puzzling. For example, when someone uses a pitching wedge and then a six-iron, how does he or she know the proper adjustment to make regarding the ball's position? Do they say to themselves, This is a six-iron, so I should move my stance approximately 2 inches to the right? How do they know this is the approximate bottom of the swing arc? The answer is that they don't. That is why I suggest that you keep the same ball position with all your irons (slightly left of the center).

Many golfers don't realize that the ball's position is relative to the body's position, not the position of the feet. For example, spread your feet about 12 inches and position the ball in the center. If someone were to see you in this position, they would say that the ball is in the center of your stance. Now assume the same position, only this time move your right foot 6 inches more to the right. If someone were now to view your stance, they would say that the ball is left of the center. However, the ball's

POWER TIP
*Beginning-to-
intermediate golfers
should play their
irons in the same
approximate
position—slightly left
of the center. Playing
the ball more toward
the right foot
promotes club-head
throwaway (casting),
which leads to a loss
of power.*

position in respect to the body's remains the same. Repeat this exercise, only on the second setup, instead of moving your right foot to the right, move both feet to the right about 4 inches. Now the ball is truly positioned left of the center because your body and feet have moved to the right.

When a golfer makes a short swing, she will usually place her feet closer together without realizing it. Since the subconscious knows that there is no need for balance on such a shot, it narrows the stance. When this occurs, the ball is not really in the center of the stance; it just appears as such because the feet are so close together. What makes the ball position centered is its relationship to the upper body. The best way to make sure that your upper body adjusts with the feet's position is to make sure that your weight is equally distributed between the right and left foot at your address position. If this is the case, when the ball is positioned anywhere from the left to right foot, it will be in its true position.

The Head's Position in the Power Stance

This question always arises: Should the head be positioned over or behind the ball? The answer really does not relate to the head as it does to the ball's position.

When you are in your power stance, your head should not tilt to the right or the left, nor should it be on a horizontal tilt, faced down, bent at the neck. The head should stay in a fairly straight alignment with your spinal column. So if the ball is positioned in the center of your stance, your head would be directly over the ball. However, with the ball positioned slightly left of the center, your head would be behind or slightly to the right of the ball. Conversely, when the ball is positioned right of the center, your head, of course, will be in front or left of the ball. With the ball in a normal left-of-center stance, you should feel that your head is behind the ball, and at the top of your backswing, you should be looking at the back of the ball.

Your head is where your visual center is located, and because of this, problems can arise. If my eyes were not located in my head, my head would be of little concern in my game. When I correctly address the ball, my head would simply stay in a fairly straight line with the spinal column and would not tilt horizontally to either the right or the left. Yet, because of my eyes, I immediately want to either stare at the ball, or I become overly conscious of my head's position.

As I have said, if your head were not your visual center, it would probably not affect your swing. But when your head moves, so does the weight of your body. This manipulation of weight can be to your advantage by enabling you to hit different-trajectory shots. For example, if at the address you move your head off to the right, your weight will naturally move to the right. This, coupled with positioning the ball forward in your stance, will enable you to hit a high-trajectory shot. If you desire a lower-trajectory shot, you would move the ball back in your stance (which immediately places the head in front or to the left of the ball), and you'll probably put a little weight on your left foot (which, of course, means that the head moves even farther to the left).

Thus, your head's position at the address will have an important impact on your swing and, of course, the resultant shot. Remember, the fact that your head houses your visual center makes it interfere with the golf swing. So let's try to position it as naturally and relaxed as the rest of your body. And to think, you thought your head was just a place to hang your hat.

Breasts and the Stance

The most frequently asked question by female students is "At the address, how should my arms be positioned in relation to my breasts?" The answer to this question varies with the woman's breast size and arm length. You have to remember that the stance should enable the arms to swing freely on the backswing. I would rarely advise a woman to put her arms next to her breasts, engulfing them. Usually, your arms cannot swing freely from this position. You might be more comfortable letting the left bicep rest on the upper portion of your left breast. Your arms should hang vertically; however, they should not be below; rather, they should extend above the breast line. Also, when bending at your hip joint, do not make the back stiff and straight. This will encourage your breasts to hang vertically, which will interfere with your arms. Instead, slightly round your shoulders. This will force your breasts in more toward your body.

If you have very large breasts and short arms, you are in trouble. Because your arms will not be able to swing freely on the backswing, the wrong parts of your body will be forced to initiate the backswing, making it very difficult to get back to the ball. A woman with large breasts and short arms will usually have a roundhouse swing that results in a topped or thin shot. (Topped and thin both mean hitting the top half of the ball, but a topped shot will simply roll on the ground while a thin shot will have a lower-than-normal trajectory.) My only suggestion is to find some means of reducing your breast size. Often just losing a few pounds or finding the right bra helps enormously.

A woman's breast size and arm length can vary dramatically. Some women will find that their breasts get in the way; others will not be concerned about their breasts. If you are just starting golf and your breasts are a problem at the address, don't worry. This is fairly normal. It just feels uncomfortable at first. However, if the discomfort should continue, you will probably have to adjust your setup. Just be aware that the arms should swing freely, without your breasts creating too much of an obstacle.

Physical attributes between women and men differ. Some are more conducive to the golf swing, some less. However, rarely have I seen a woman unable to play a decent round of golf solely because of her breast size. Do not let anyone tell you because you have breasts that golf is not your game. This could not be further from the truth.

Segmentation

It is important that you understand the role of segmenting (bending) your body at the address. By segmenting, I mean what previously worked as one unit now functions as two. For example, when you stand erect, your entire body functions as a unit. When you turn your upper body, it is natural for your lower body to turn in unison. However, when you bend from your hips (as you would when addressing a golf ball), you create a distinction between your upper and lower body. Now when you turn, there will be less unison between the two halves. This is an important concept because this segmentation causes the use of different muscles, which can help you execute different shots. Let's say that when you putt, you have been told that your body appears to move on your backstroke. An adjustment in your stance so that you segment your body by bending from as many joints as possible should provide the cure. When I set up to my putt, I bend from my hips, knees, and elbows, creating a three-part segmentation, which will lessen the likelihood that on my backstroke my body will move with the putter.

This segmentation is also important for isolating any part of your body that you want to use less or more. Let's say I have the type of putting stroke guided by my shoulders. To better enable my shoulders to function, I would want to bend at my hips (or stomach) and knees but leave my wrists and elbows fairly straight. Bending at the hips (or stomach) allows the shoulders to move independently of the lower body. By permitting very little bending of the elbows and wrists, the putting-stroke path will come directly from my shoulders.

The stance that we assume at the address is built on this theory of segmentation. At the address, we want our body segmented correctly to enable our power anchors to fulfill their roles. We also want the club's face pointed toward our target and our power anchors aligned to create a proper path for the backswing. Once situated as such, we are ready to start our backswing.

4

The Power Backswing

The backswing is often incorrectly viewed as a windup. During a windup you tense and contort your body to create leverage. In the golf swing, it is the club's backswing position that will help to create power. There is some twisting and contorting of the body on the backswing. However, to feel contorted should be a by-product of correct club placement, not a golfer's goal.

I am sure all of you have at one point in time been told that if you just had more of a shoulder or hip turn on your backswing, the ball would go farther. Watch out. It is precisely this advice that will lead you to lose, not gain, distance. Remember, the golf swing is based on technique, not muscle, and it is important, particularly on the backswing, to keep this in mind. Now that we realize that the idea is to place our body in a specific position, let us see what that position is and how it will affect our power factors.

Once you have assumed your address posture, you are ready to exe-

FIGURE 20. The shoulders initiate the backswing.

cute the backswing. On the backswing, the movement of your torso and lower body should be dependent on the turning of your shoulders. The shoulders should initiate the backswing, and when the swing is completed, the shoulders should be turned approximately 90 degrees. The posture that you established at the address should be maintained on the backswing, and the shoulders should neither dip nor raise (see Fig. 20). Once the shoulders begin to turn, the lower body should respond to the upper body's movement. This means the hips will begin to turn; when the swing is completed, the hips will have turned about 45 degrees. As previously stated, your lower body should function as a base upon which your upper body turns.

The Power Center

Place your left hand on the center of your chest, resting by the bottom of your collarbone. This is your center, the motor of the golf swing. On the backswing your center will turn 90 degrees away from the ball, and on the downswing, it will move 180 degrees or more from its backswing position toward the target (see Figs. 21 and 22). One of the most common errors on the

POWER TIP

At the top of your backswing you should not feel that you are staring directly over the ball. This will mean that your power center has not completed its backswing rotation. Instead, you should feel as though you are looking at the back of the ball. This should ensure full rotation on the backswing.

FIGURE 21. At the top of the backswing, the power center has turned 90 degrees.

FIGURE 22. From its backswing position, the power center will rotate 180 degrees to the swing's finish.

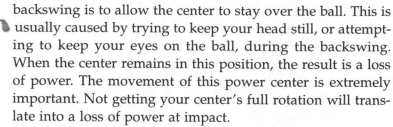

backswing is to allow the center to stay over the ball. This is usually caused by trying to keep your head still, or attempting to keep your eyes on the ball, during the backswing. When the center remains in this position, the result is a loss of power. The movement of this power center is extremely important. Not getting your center's full rotation will translate into a loss of power at impact.

On the backswing the average complete shoulder turn is about 90 degrees. Some golfers, depending on their flexibility, will turn more or less. Generally speaking, a turn greater than 90 degrees tends to throw the body and club out of position. Again place your left hand on your center. You will know that you have turned your center correctly if at the top of your backswing the back of your left hand is in near alignment with your right side (see Fig. 23).

FIGURE 23. The back of the left hand is in straight alignment with the right leg.

The Weight Transfer on the Backswing

As the power center turns to the right, the weight will shift from a 50:50 left-foot/right-foot distribution at the address to a 40:60 left-foot/right-foot ratio at the top of the backswing. This weight shift should not be done intentionally; rather, it should be a result of the power center's movement. In order for this weight shift to occur, the right knee must remain flexed (although it does straighten slightly from the address position). If the right knee does not stay bent, this will lead to a reverse weight shift, sometimes called a reverse pivot (see Fig. 24).

Power Anchors on the Backswing

Your hips act as your primary power anchor. As such, they provide a base on which your upper body can effectively coil. By the top of the backswing, the hips should have turned about 45 degrees. This turn should not be initiated by the hips but because the shoulders have forced them to turn. You do not want the hips to initiate the backswing.

There are two motions that you do not want the hips to execute on the backswing. First, you do not want them to turn in unison with the shoulders; second, you do not want to keep them too still. True, they should be anchored, but they still will turn approximately 45 degrees.

FIGURE 24. The reverse pivot. Notice how the right knee has straightened.

As I have stated, the lower body should act as a base upon which your upper body turns. This means that the left heel should remain on the ground during the backswing. On the backswing, smaller muscles require more precision and are important in positioning the club.

The turning shoulders should dictate the backswing path for the club and arms. Once the shoulders begin to turn, the arms will simply follow their path. As the arms are swinging, the wrists will begin their 90-degree vertical cock, which will form the power angle.

Creating the Power Angle on the Backswing

When you address the ball, your power angle is already partially set. Your wrists are not in a straight line with the forearms, but are bent at a 45-degree angle. With the club gripped correctly, the heel of your left hand is on top of the club's shaft and lies in the hand's fingers. This proper grip will ensure that the power angle is set correctly.

When your shoulders begin to turn, you can start to cock your wrists (set your power angle). Ideally, we want the left hand to initiate and force both wrists to cock. The wrists should cock vertically (see Fig. 25).

FIGURE 25. Once the shoulders begin to turn, the wrists should start to cock vertically.

POWER TIP

Many women have a tendency to throw their hips into the backswing (make them turn with the shoulders). Often it is because they incorrectly believe that the hips are a direct source of power. But the hips are an indirect source of power. Their 45-degree turn, compared to the shoulders' 90-degree turn, creates a coiling effect. This coil is not created when the hips initiate the turn on the backswing.

POWER TIP

Many women are told to force their weight to shift to the right on their backswing. This will usually lead to a sway. You should never have to force the weight shift. If your center turns correctly and the right knee remains flexed, this shift will happen naturally. Something happening naturally in the golf swing means one less problem to worry about!

POWER TIP
Many women are afraid to cock their wrists too early in fear of picking up the club. As long as your shoulders are turning, the club cannot be picked up. Only when the shoulders are not in motion is it possible for the hands to pick up the club.

POWER TIP
Do not press downward with the heel of your left hand to cock your wrists on the backswing. This will pull your left shoulder down, which will cause your head to dip.

FIGURE 26. A rear view of the power assembly, which includes the cocked wrists and bent right elbow, both of which form 90-degree angles.

Take your club and with extended arms hold it so that your arms and the club's shaft are parallel to the ground. The club's butt should now point directly back toward the center of your stomach. Next, bend your wrists so that the club's shaft points directly toward the sky; the butt of the club will now be perpendicular to the ground. Repeat this motion several times. This is the manner in which your wrists cock on the backswing. Now assume this position and turn your shoulders to the right. Let your hands rise to about ear level and place the shaft of the club so that it is parallel to the ground. This is the top of your backswing.

Now, assume your address position and allow your wrists to cock and hands to swing to about ear level. Once your shoulders begin to turn, you will have the top of your backswing.

Creating the Power Assembly

As your wrists cock, you will notice that your right elbow will begin to fold. You want to be sure that the right elbow does not fold until the wrists have begun to cock. At the top of your swing, the right elbow should point toward, and the bicep should be parallel, or slightly below parallel, to the ground (see Fig. 24).

At the top of the backswing, your hands should remain extended from your body. If you are right-handed, the left arm will be fairly straight at this point. It is important that the straightness of the left arm be a combined product of the right arm extending and a proper grip, not of tension (Fig. 26). If you have gripped the club correctly, with the heel of the left hand on top of the club (see chapter 2), initiating the wrist cock with the left hand will automatically straighten your left arm by the top of the swing. You can even bow the left arm at the top of the swing. However, you do not want the elbow to break. This straight left arm combined with the turned shoulders, cocked wrists, and bent right elbow form our power assembly (see Fig. 26). It is the speed and maintenance of this assembly that will create power on the downswing.

The Swing Path

To understand what is meant by swing path, stand directly behind a golfer's right side. Notice the path the arms and club take during the swing. This is called the swing path. The correct backswing path places the club in a position that will enable it to return on the proper downswing path. A good golf swing can take an unusual backswing path and through compensations on the downswing still result in a good shot. However, it is advisable to place the club in the most convenient position possible for it to return to the golf ball.

The three different paths the club can take on the backswing are square, flat, and upright. The square path is generally considered ideal, although everyone has a different ideal path relative to their body size. The shoulders establish a golfer's swing path. If the hands swing on the same plane as the shoulders, when the shoulders complete their 90-degree turn, the hands and club will be on the perfect path. The only problem is that the hands have more distance to travel than the turning shoulders. When the hands move at the same speed as the shoulders, after the shoulders complete their 90-degree turn, the hands are left in about a half-swing position. Ideally, we want the hands to rise to about ear level. As the shoulders turn, the wrists should cock vertically. Since the hands should move faster than the turning shoulders, the hands should have traveled one-quarter of their distance when the shoulders have turned one-

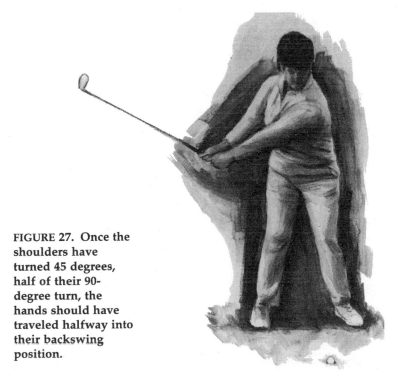

FIGURE 27. Once the shoulders have turned 45 degrees, half of their 90-degree turn, the hands should have traveled halfway into their backswing position.

POWER TIP

If you try to use tension to keep your left arm straight on the backswing, you will make it difficult for your wrists to cock and set the power angle.

POWER TIP

If you have a chronic problem with your left elbow bending on your backswing, check to see that your right elbow is not hinging first. This will pull your left arm toward your body and cause it to break at the elbow. Remember that when the shoulders begin to turn, the left wrist, not the right elbow, will be the first to hinge on the backswing.

POWER TIP

Visualizing keeping your right elbow by your side will usually force the left arm to break. Allow your right elbow to swing freely on the backswing; however, do not let it chicken-wing (point toward the sky). Make sure the elbow points toward the ground.

quarter of their complete turn. When the shoulders have turned 45 degrees (half) of their 90-degree turn, the hands should be halfway into position (see Fig. 27). Of course, when the shoulders have made their full turn, the hands should have reached the top of their backswing position. Ideally, if the arms and hands are going to follow the same path as the shoulders, they should never be in motion without the shoulders also being in motion. Movement of the arms and hands without the shoulders turning is called "picking up the club." Picking up the club will usually alter the club's backswing path so that the shoulder and club plane will differ.

Movement of the swing path on a more horizontal plane than the shoulders (around the body) is called a flat swing path. There are, of course, varying degrees of flat. You might hear a golf professional or a sports commentator say, "Her swing looks a little flat," or, "He has a slightly flat swing." This is not necessarily bad. It is just that their swing path deviates slightly from the square swing path. As I previously stated, the backswing path can vary from the norm if there are compensations for this variance on the downswing. However, the greater the degree of variance, the greater the chance for making a mistake. A very flat swing can also be called a roundhouse swing. In a roundhouse motion your swing is so flat that you are literally swinging around your body on both the back and downswing. This type of swing generally produces a very weak slice or a pull to the left. There is usually very little chance for the club to get on the correct downswing path with this type of swing.

An upright swing plane means that the club has traveled on a plane that is more vertical than the square plane and as a result the hands will be in a higher position. Again, there are varying degrees of upright swings. With a very flat swing you are usually forced to make an outside-to-inside downswing. This type of motion commonly produces a slice (which is a very weak shot). With an upright swing plane, two motions could occur on the downswing. First, the club could take an outside-to-inside swing path (similar to our flat downswing plane), or the club could fall onto our square swing plane. Many good golfers swing the club back on a slightly upright swing plane and at the top of their backswing; when the club changes direction, it drops slightly into the square plane. This type of swing can be very effective in producing power. Conversely, when someone's swing has become too upright, the steepness of this plane will produce a very descending blow to the ball. A descending blow to a tee shot will result in a popped shot, in which the shot's height is almost equal to its length.

You might ask why one's swing plane becomes either too flat or too upright. There can be several reasons why, but let me give you one of the most common reasons. For an upright swing this can mean that the hands have pushed away from the body on the backswing. This is usually the cause of a faulty swing thought (a mental image used by a golfer to picture an aspect of her golf swing), such as dragging the club head on the backswing or taking the club straight back. For a flat swing, it can be the natural desire of the hands to want to swing around the body with the shoulders. As I have stated, backswing paths may vary among good golfers. Whatever our swing path may be, if it enables a correct downswing, then it has done its job.

The Effects of a Woman's Breasts on the Swing Path

One of the primary concerns about women and golf is the role of the breasts in the golf swing. It has been said that because of our bustline it is difficult for us to maintain the proper swing path. The first problem with this theory is that in order for it to be correct it must assume that all women have the same-size breasts. Through my years of teaching experience I have found that men and women alike come in a variety of shapes and sizes. I will agree that a woman with an extremely large bustline and short arms is at a disadvantage in executing the golf swing. But I would also argue that a rotund man with enlarged breasts and short arms is also at a disadvantage, and I think you will find it more common that beer bellies, rather than breasts, interfere with the club's swing path.

One concern seems to be that once the shoulders start to turn, the arms cannot swing fast enough or on the correct plane because of the woman's breasts. What most critics do not realize or fail to mention is that even in fairly large-breasted women (assuming that there is ample arm length), the breasts are not in the way once the shoulders have turned about 60 degrees. At this point, the shoulder turn should have moved the breasts far enough to the right so as not to interfere with the swinging arms (again assuming a fairly balanced body proportion).

I think the problem emerges when men, not having breasts, claim to have knowledge of the hindrances that breasts cause in the golf swing. Beginning female golfers will often complain that the backswing feels uncomfortable because their breasts are in

POWER TIP

On the backswing, women are often told to implement a one-piece take-away. This conjures up a picture of the shoulders, arms, and club swinging back in a uniform motion. But this concept is incorrect and is usually the most common cause of overswinging. The arms must swing faster than the turning shoulders to get into their position. By the time the shoulders have reached their 90-degree turn, the power angle should be set and ready to swing back to the ball.

POWER TIP

Trying to keep the left arm straight on the backswing can force the club to take an outside path. Try relaxing your left arm at the address and allow the hinging of the wrists to put the club into position.

the way, and many male professionals will reinforce that notion. But the problem is not that your breasts are a hindrance. Rather, it is that you are not used to performing an athletic feat where your breasts are so involved in the sport's technique. I cannot think of another sport that requires the arms to be in a position of such symmetry that the breasts are actually involved. Once you become accustomed to the golf swing, the feeling of discomfort about your breasts will disappear (assuming you are making the correct address and backswing) to the point that you really don't notice them (except in cases of weight gain).

A golfer once came to me in a panic. She loved the game of golf, but she had been told by a golf professional that her breast size would impede improvement. Her breasts were unusually large for her physique. However, she had very long arms, which created ample compensation for her breasts, so it was obvious that the problem lay with her swing, not her physique. After watching her take several practice swings, I noticed that she had an extremely flat swing plane. I questioned her as to what her swing thoughts were on the backswing. She replied that in the past she had problems with a "flying" right elbow. Consequently, her golf pro had told her to keep her elbow in by her side during the backswing. This was her problem! First of all, the right elbow should never remain at your side during the backswing. The elbow swings out and away from your torso. Attempting to keep the elbow in at her side had forced her to swing the club around her body (on a flat swing plane). This, coupled with her large breast size, complicated the problem. Consequently, the arms did not swing freely after their 60-degree shoulder turn. They were inhibited by her breasts and could not generate any speed. I corrected her swing plane and explained the cause of her flying right elbow. Within four lessons she had added 10 yards of distance to each club.

The moral of the story: Never let anyone tell you that because of your breasts you cannot swing the golf club correctly; except in extreme cases it just isn't so. If your breasts are causing problems on the backswing, it is more likely a problem with your swing, not your bustline!

Overswinging in the Quest for Power

The most common problem seen in a woman's backswing is overswinging, or exaggerating the role of a particular part of her anatomy during the backswing. This is common with women because it is the natural way that the body tries to generate power. In most sports this method would work, but in golf it doesn't. The backswing is for position; it is not a windup. The more you overswing, the more likely it is that you will lose the power angle on your downswing. Overswinging can occur with any part of your anatomy. The hips, legs, shoulders, and arms all will have this tendency. You have to convince yourself that if you swing the club into the proper position on the backswing, you will have sufficient momentum to generate club-head speed on the downswing.

The Power Turn

As we have seen on the backswing, the shoulders should make a 90-degree turn. Making a greater shoulder turn would appear to give the upper body more torque and consequently generate greater power, but unfortunately this is not the case. With too much shoulder turn on the backswing, chances are you will upset one of the other power factors that will be essential in hitting the ball squarely. One possible problem is that you can turn your center too far, which will throw your weight out of balance (a reverse pivot). With too much shoulder turn, your club's position on the backswing is also affected, making it more difficult for the club head to be delivered squarely to the ball. A factor that is frequently overlooked is how the shoulders should turn.

The shoulder turn on the backswing should put your power center into motion. When the shoulders have turned 90 degrees, the power center is ready to turn 180 degrees forward into its follow-through. When viewing the backswing, most golfers will notice that the left shoulder cap appears to turn down and under the chin. Although this seems to be the case, the reality is that the shoulders are simply turning level. It is the axis on which they are turning that is tilted. Consequently, on your backswing, you never want to intentionally force your shoulder under your chin. This will lead to the head dipping (moving downward) on the backswing. Dipping will not only move your body downward; it will also prevent your power center from making its correct backswing rotation.

In chapter 3, we discussed how the upper body should be inclined at a 45-degree tilt in the stance. Stand straight and turn your shoulders 90 degrees to the right. Now make a 45-degree

POWER TIP

One of the best ways to combat overswinging is to make sure the heel of your left foot remains on the ground during the backswing. This helps secure your power anchors.

POWER TIP

Seeing the club in your peripheral vision at the top of your backswing does not always indicate an overswing. Often this is a result of the wrists hinging too late (at the top of, rather than during, the backswing) on the backswing. In this situation, try cocking your wrists a little earlier in your backswing.

POWER TIP

It is a common belief among golfers that in order to generate power it is necessary for the shoulders to turn as far as possible. You must always remember that the backswing is for positioning, not power. A 90-degree shoulder turn is sufficient for most golf swings.

POWER TIP

Many golfers believe that on the backswing the shoulders should turn under their chins, but that isn't the case. In fact, the shoulders should turn on a level plane, in relation to the upper body's degree of tilt at the address.

tilt and turn your shoulders. You will notice you did nothing different with your shoulders; it was your tilt at a 45-degree angle that dictated your shoulder plane.

This time, intentionally force your shoulder under your chin and allow your head to dip. Notice what happens to your power center. It is unable to make its full rotation. The power center is the motor of the golf swing. If it does not make a complete turn, a loss of power will result. Ideally, once we are set in our posture at the address, we want to maintain it through the backswing. It should not be altered by the shoulders turning downward or, conversely, lifting on the backswing.

The Shoulders and the Power Center

The shoulders and power center can be viewed as one unit with two different functions. Obviously, the shoulders and power center are connected, so when the shoulders turn, the power center is set in motion. As we have seen, the power center's rotation is the motor of our swing. The power center is not connected to the arms, but the shoulders are. This creates two roles for the shoulders. The first is to put the power center in motion; the second, to govern the arms' and clubs' backswing path. Any movement by the shoulders will affect the power center; conversely, any movement by the power center will affect the shoulders.

FIGURE 28. The wrists are slightly cupped, and the club face is at a 45-degree angle, which is a square position. If the club face were parallel to the ground, its position would be closed. If the club face is perpendicular to the ground it is open.

The Position of the Wrists and Club Head at the Top of the Backswing

At the top of the backswing, the club head can assume one of three positions: open, square, or closed (see Fig. 28). An open club-face position means that the club face is perpendicular to the ground. A square position is when the club face is tilted at a 45-degree angle. A closed club face occurs when the club's bottom edge runs parallel to the ground at a 90-degree angle to the open position. The left wrist can also assume three different positions: cupped, flat, and pronated. (The left wrist is convexed.) These wrist positions usually, but not always, complement the club-face position—a cupped position can produce an open club face, a flat wrist position can create a square club face, and a pronated wrist can produce a closed club face at the top of the backswing.

The club head's backswing position will depend on the manner in which the club was gripped at the address and how the wrists cock on the backswing. The farther the club is gripped into the palm of the left hand, the flatter the wrist bone of the left hand at the top of the backswing. Conversely, the more the club head is placed into the fingers of the left hand, the more cupped the back of the left wrist will be.

At the address, the more the club is gripped toward the palms of your hands, the more the club face will be in an open position at the top of the backswing. If your club is gripped correctly with the heel of the left hand on top of the club's shaft, the club face will be more square at the top of the backswing. Remember that this occurs in varying degrees. Keep in mind that the club face's position between open and square can equal anywhere from a 0- to a 45-degree angle. Holding the club too far into the palm of the right hand can create a closed position.

We have seen how the grip position affects the club-face position. The next determining factor will be how the wrists cock. The wrist positions that we have discussed have been predicated on the idea that the wrists are cocking vertically (as they should) on the backswing. However, let's say that instead of making their vertical hinge, the wrists cock on a more horizontal plane. When this occurs, the back of the left hand will be in a flatter position, and the club face will be closed. If the wrists cock more vertically than normal on the backswing, the club face will be put into a very open position.

Ideally, the club face should be square to the target (pointing toward the target) at impact. This means that at the top of our backswing the club face should be in a position that, when swung correctly on the downswing, will be square at impact. Remember the rotation of the power center; the club head's rotation will be similar. When the power center turns to the right, the back of the club's toe will point toward the sky. This is a square position. As the power center turns back toward the ball, the club head will follow, so that at impact, when the power center is pointing in the vicinity of the ball, the club face will be pointing down the target line. Conversely, when the power center turns to the left on the follow-through, once again the front of the club head's toe will point toward the sky (see Fig. 29). From square to square to square is the ideal path for the

POWER TIP

The club face is in an open position when, at the top of the backswing, the club's bottom is at a 90-degree angle to the ground. If the club should open more than 90 degrees, a tremendous loss of power at impact will result.

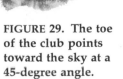

FIGURE 29. The toe of the club points toward the sky at a 45-degree angle.

club head to travel. When the power center turns toward the right and the club face is square, if the wrists are hinged (cocked) in a vertical manner, the club face remains square (at about a 45-degree tilt to the ground). Now, let's say that the wrists do not hinge vertically but cock more horizontally. This will place the club head in more of a closed position (open being 0 degrees; closed, 90 degrees). If the downswing follows the power center, as in the previous example, instead of the club face being square at impact, it will be closed (pointing toward the left). The resulting flight path of the ball would also be to the left. So unless there is some compensation on the downswing, the club face is destined to be in a closed position at impact. For this reason, the ideal club position is square, with the back of the left wrist slightly cupped. This is the easiest manner for the club head to travel on the downswing with the least amount of compensations, thus creating more club-head speed.

The Club's Shaft

If you have gripped the club correctly, at the top of your backswing the club's shaft may not be parallel to the ground; rather it may point slightly toward the ground. This is not necessarily incorrect; it may be due to your grip. When the heel of the left hand rests on top of the club's shaft, the completed wrist cock will usually result in the shaft of the club pointing slightly toward the ground. Again, this is not incorrect. It simply relates to your hand's position on the club. Many great golfers have had the club point past parallel on their backswing. However, the club's traveling past parallel for other reasons would be considered an overswing. Realize that the shaft pointing past parallel may be a by-product of your grip.

The Power Press

Creating a repetitive golf swing from a completely stationary address position is very difficult, if not impossible. All good golfers use a motion known as a forward press to initiate the backswing. A slight press forward (toward your target) acts as a trigger to swing backward. The forward press also helps you establish a tempo for your swing. All good golfers have a forward press, and these presses can vary dramatically. Some golfers may simply increase grip pressure in their left hand, while others may swivel their head and kick their right knee in toward the ball. One thing you must remember about a forward press is that whatever part of your anatomy you press forward, that part will most likely be the fastest to swing back. Let's say that your hands are slow to cock on the backswing. You might want to press your hands slightly toward your target on your take-away, making them react faster on the backswing. The forward press should be a very subtle movement. When you press forward, you want to make sure you do not change your body or the club's position.

I once had a student who had a chronic problem of swinging the club outside the normal path on her backswing. She had been to many professionals and could not determine why this would happen. Her forward press was what I call a left-sided press. Before the take-away she would slightly press her entire left side toward her target. She had been doing this for a while, and it seemed to put her in a nice rhythm. However, I noticed that on her forward press, instead of pressing toward her target, she was now moving her shoulder and her hips slightly to the left. This subtle movement changed her address position and her backswing path. I replaced her old forward press with one that did not involve so much body movement. Within the week, the problem was resolved, and she had her old swing back! So you see, as much as a forward press can help you, it is important to make it as subtle as possible so as not to affect your body's or club's position.

Tempo and the Forward Press

Another function of the forward press is to put your body into a rhythm, or tempo. A typical tempo count for a golf swing is one, two, and three, where the "and" is a slight hesitation and the forward press is your one count. The two is your backswing, the "and" is a pause created by the change of direction at the top of your backswing, and the three is your downswing. This one-two-and-three can assume different speeds. For example, your swing may be one-twoooo-and-three or oooone-two-aaaand-three. Tempos will vary as much as the individuals who use them.

I have heard it said that you can tell a lot about a person's personality by the speed of her golf swing, and from my experiences I believe this to be true. A slow, methodical person will tend to have a rather slow, methodical tempo. A faster, more aggressive person will tend to swing quickly, often not even per-

POWER TIP

Be sure that you do not swing the club too slowly on the backswing. A backswing that is too slow creates a tremendous amount of tension, which culminates at the top of the swing. This tension will cause you to "jump" (hurry) on your downswing, which will force an early release of the power assembly and result in a loss of power.

mitting the "and" in her swing. The easy, laid-backed person usually has a big, flowing, loose motion, what I refer to as a spaghetti swing. If a person conducts everything in her life at a certain speed and in a certain manner, why should her golf swing be any different?

These are your internal bodily rhythms, and they will manifest themselves in the golf swing. All of us, from Jack Nicklaus to the novice golfer, have a predilection for certain idiosyncrasies in our swing. These idiosyncrasies are based on our physical build, muscular strength, and personalities. It is natural to want to use the strongest parts of our body when trying to generate power in the golf swing even if this is not correct. It is also natural to revert to our basic bodily rhythms even if they are incorrect. However, once we are aware wherein the problem lies, we can make the necessary adjustments. So, just because you are a fast person does not mean that your swing has to move like lightning. There are exercises you can perform to put your swing back into sync. Conversely, being a slow person does not mean that your swing must move like molasses. Something as simple as establishing a forward press can increase the speed of your backswing.

Creating a Forward Press

When creating a forward press, you must keep in mind that whatever part of your body you press forward will also be, more than likely, the fastest to move backward. For example, if you have a tendency on your backswing to pick up the club with your hands (the hands initiate the swing, not the shoulders), you might want to use a right knee kick toward the target as a forward press. However, if you have a problem with too much body movement on your backswing, then slightly pressing the hands toward your target should help.

The most common forward press is the left-hand-and-arm press. Although the shoulders may initiate the backswing, in order for the hands to reach their destination, they must travel a greater distance. To do this, the hands are going to move faster than the turning shoulders. One way this is accomplished is by slightly pressing the left arm and hand toward your target. The rebound effect of this slight press forward will give your arms and hands the speed they need to swing back into position.

To get the correct feeling of a forward press, assume your

normal address position. Stand with a wall facing your body's left side. Now lean so that your entire left side is touching the wall. Press your left side against the wall and let it rebound back into position. Do this several times. Feel the springing motion backward. After doing this enough times, you might realize that the forward press forces the muscles in certain areas of your body to contract (tense). This tension is of the constructive nature; it tells our body that we are going to attempt to create an athletic motion.

This is exactly the principle on which the forward press is based. Using this principle, you can see how various parts of your body can be used to create a rebounding effect. You can see why someone who tends to sway their body to the right on the backswing would not want to implement a forward press that involved the entire left side of his or her body.

We have already discussed the body's natural biorhythms and its innate need for tempo, because of which most golfers are unaware that they already have a forward press. You might ask a friend to look at your swing and see what type of press you have, or better yet, take a video of your swing. It is also fun to videotape swings by touring pros and notice what type of press they use. Often the press may be very subtle and can only be detected by a trained eye. You might want to take a lesson from a trained professional to identify your press. An incorrect press can be as destructive as any move in your golf swing.

Now that we have swung the club into its correct back-swing position, it is time to reverse our motion and begin our downswing. Traditionally, the golf swing has been viewed as a two-part motion, the backswing and the downswing. Because of this traditional view, an area very important is often overlooked, and that is *the change of direction.*

POWER TIP

To get an idea of the correct arm speed on the backswing, use the swinging-arms drill found in chapter 14. This is an excellent exercise and will be very helpful in improving other aspects of your golf swing.

5

The Top of the Backswing
to the Start of the Downswing

Perhaps the most crucial part of the golf swing is the top of the backswing. This is the point at which your body changes direction to return to the ball. This change of direction affects all your power factors; the swing path and club-face direction will be determined, and lag pressure will be created. This is also an essential part of the swing's timing. In chapter 4 we discussed tempo. This part of the swing is the "and" in the swing's tempo. During the change of direction a faulty backswing path can be corrected as much as a good backswing path can be altered (see Fig. 30).

The "And" and the Change of Direction

As explained in chapter 4, the "and" part of your swing's tempo is the slight hesitation between the time when your body finishes its backswing and begins its downswing. This "and" is analogous to what happens when you breathe. While breathing, you don't force air in and out in rapid succession (like a

FIGURE 30. **The change of direction is the point at which the backswing becomes the downswing.**

dog panting). Instead, there is a slight hesitation as the air reverses its flow. In golf, this hesitation enables our power assembly to get set and begin the downswing path. Also in breathing, when you are relaxed, air enters and exits your body in a smooth manner. When you panic, your breathing pattern changes, and breaths become shorter. Ideally, when you complete your backswing and change of direction, it should feel light, almost unnoticeable. However, when you get the sensation that your swing is too quick or out of sync, there usually exists a problem with the change of direction. Good mechanics can create a good tempo. The same holds true for the change of direction. A consistent, correctly executed backswing will generate a smooth change of direction. Bad mechanics can make this transition much more difficult. You can see how this change of direction is crucial to the swing's execution.

The Power Assembly and the Change of Direction

At the top of your backswing, your power assembly should be positioned and ready to begin the downswing (see page 14). The right elbow should be bent (not cocked), with your hands extended from your body. It is essential for your power assembly to stay intact during this change of direction.

POWER TIP

One of the most common problems that occurs during the change of directions is the right elbow taking an active role in initiating the downswing instead of the elbow hinging on the backswing. Often the elbow, not the wrists, will cock (see Fig. 31). Thus, when the change of direction occurs, the elbow springs from its position and creates a casting motion. When this occurs, the power assembly is destroyed, and the swing's efficiency is diminished.

FIGURE 31. The elbows, not the wrists, have cocked.

During the change of direction, many golfers attempt to force their right elbow into their side. This is not necessary. If you keep your power assembly together on the downswing, you will notice that the elbow does this naturally. Intentionally pushing your elbow toward your side will disrupt your downswing path.

POWER TIP
The hips are often viewed as a source of power and are thus responsible for the power assembly's initial movement and consequential increases in speed. Do not try to generate power with your hips. Their job is to respond to the assembly's movement and clear out of the way. In the process, they do increase the speed of the assembly; however, I repeat, it is only in response to the assembly's movement. Your hips should never initiate the downswing.

FIGURE 32. The arms and hands will move on the same approximate swing path on the downswing as in the backswing.

The first move that will initiate the start of the downswing is the power assembly moving on an arc back to the ball. It is important that when this power assembly returns toward the ball, its return plane is on an arc (see Fig. 32). Instead of visualizing the entire power assembly moving at once, you might want to visualize the hands returning on this arc, with the other parts of the assembly, such as the right elbow, staying intact.

Once your assembly begins to move on its arc, the body will naturally get out of its way. The hips and lower body will respond to the power assembly by increasing their speed in proportion to the assembly's increasing speed.

Also during the change of direction, your weight will transfer from your right foot to your left (assuming that your backswing position is correct). Again, this is in response to the power assembly moving along its arc. This can be likened to throwing a ball or performing any athletic move that involves forward motion. It is not natural for the weight to move in an opposite direction in response to the hands' and arms' forward momentum.

Lag Pressure

It is at this point in the swing that lag pressure (see chapter 1) begins to build. The speed of the power assembly, combined with its maintenance (staying intact), creates greater lag pressure. Lag pressure eventually translates into club-head speed. Any incorrect movement that occurs in the change of direction that causes the power assembly to disassemble will result in a release of lag pressure and a subsequent loss of power.

The Power Accelerator

We have already discussed the wrist cock in the chapter on the backswing. However, this element needs to be further developed in regard to the change of direction. In some swings the power angle is set and ready to attack the ball at or by the top of the backswing. In others, the wrists do not fully cock by the time they reach their backswing position, but instead finish cocking on their downswing. This downswing cocking motion is what is referred to as the power accelerator because it builds up tremendous club-head lag pressure. With this type of swing, the hinge and the release of the hands feel almost as one. The result is a powerful, effortless shot. It is this power accelerator that can give distance to a swing regardless of the golfer's strength. The average golfer should not attempt to create this power accelerator. Rather, just be aware that the additional hinging on the downswing can produce a disproportionate amount of power (in regard to strength). The best way to create the power accelerator is to work on the fundamentals already discussed in this book. For example, there is no way you can incorporate the power accelerator into your swing if your right elbow cocks before your wrists on the backswing. And very importantly, if you do not have the correct grip, it is almost impossible for the power accelerator to work in your swing.

Plane Shifters

Plane shifters are any part of your anatomy that forces the downswing or backswing planes to change. Plane shifting is not necessarily a bad motion. It usually takes place at the change of direction from backswing to downswing. This shifting can also occur on the backswing and might appear as a loop as the backswing starts on one plane and shifts to another by the top of the swing. Most swing planes shift slightly from their backswing planes to the downswing plane. Plane shifting on the backswing is not nearly as common as it is on the downswing. Whereas the arms and wrists are usually the cause of backswing plane shifting, the most commonly used plane shifters on the downswing are the legs, hips, and shoulders.

Plane shifting with the legs: A strong leg drive will pull the lower body toward the target. That the upper body lags behind usually forces the arms and hands to take a slightly lower downswing path.

Plane shifting with the hips: When a strong hip turn initiates the downswing, two different results can occur: The strong spin can force the arms and hands on a more inside to outside path, or the spinning hips can force the shoulders to spin, which creates an outside-to-inside downswing path.

Plane shifting with the shoulders: If the shoulders initiate the downswing by turning, the club will be forced on an outside-to-inside downswing path. This is frequently referred to as "coming over the top." If the shoulders do not turn but drop downward on the downswing, the swing plane will shift to an inside-to-outside path.

Plane shifting is very frequent, and the most common shift is for the plane to return to the ball on a slightly higher arc (more outside to inside). Keep in mind that plane shifting occurs in degrees. A golfer can still have an inside-to-outside downswing path and have shifted her plane to a higher arc (more outside). She can also do the opposite by having an outside swing plane and shift to the inside and still be outside the target line.

Misfiring and the Domino Effect

We have discussed the analogy that one's tempo can be likened to pistons firing in an engine. The most crucial time for those pistons to stay in harmony is at the top of the backswing. But what if one of these pistons misfires?

Let's say that the hips, not the power assembly, initiate the downswing. For a golfer who is used to her power assembly starting her downswing, this is equivalent to a piston misfiring. This jump-start with the hips will cause the lower body to move much faster than the torso, which, in turn, will create a domino effect in the golf swing, with one movement in the swing affecting the next, and so on. For example, if the hips move too quickly, the arms cannot swing fast enough to square the club face to the ball. This results in a subconscious attempt to deliver the club head quickly by casting the club. Upon casting the club, the golfer will have to lift herself out of her posture; otherwise, the club head will hit the ground. When this occurs, the head is lifted, and because the club head is still unable to square its path, the club face remains open, and the ball veers toward the right. The hip's jump-starting could be likened to the first domino falling, and after that the other dominoes' fate is sealed. So you can see how a misfiring of one piston can send the whole works into a frenzy.

The Mechanics of Timing

Do good mechanics produce good timing, or is it timing that produces the mechanics of a good swing? The answer is both. However, ideally, mechanics should produce our sense of timing. If you execute all the correct mechanics on the backswing and your downswing execution is perfect, we would say that your timing is perfect. However, a golfer is only human, and being perfect in the game of golf is something that for many is rarely witnessed. This is where timing reaches an almost spiritual or subconscious level.

Great golfers have an innate sense of timing that is impeccable. In a split second their bodies can adjust and compensate for slight variations in bodily movements, ensuring a fluid swing motion. Which is where hours on the practice range and the development of an internal sense of rhythm come into play. It also could be described as concentration, the ability to blot out most conscious actions so that the body can perform its role in creating the golf swing. Whatever you want to call it, timing basically determines whether your swing is on or off. As I have stated, good mechanics will create good timing. Some golfers will internalize this timing (be able to repeat it even when the swing mechanics are not good), and some will not. It is this process of internalization that will separate the better or worse of two golfers that both have mechanically excellent golf swings. The mind likes order, and whether you realize it or not, your body establishes certain hidden rhythms. One of these hidden

POWER TIP

Golfers are often taught to lift their left heel on the backswing and to replant the heel to initiate the downswing. Sometimes a slight lift of the left heel is acceptable (usually for top amateur or professional players), forced by the backswing. This lifting should not be done in an attempt to acquire power in a swing. In the majority of cases, it disrupts the backswing position and jars the downswing. A swing based on lifting and replanting the left heel is one based on timing rather than mechanics. It is my suggestion to any amateur golfer not to lift the left heel on the backswing with the idea of replanting it to obtain power. The jarring action of replanting the foot can cause the power assembly to break down.

POWER TIP

You should never feel a dramatic increase in the club head's speed at impact. If you are swinging the club correctly, you will feel your power assembly accelerating at about the shoulder-to-mid-waist level. The club's impact should feel smooth and effortless. If you do feel your hands hitting or slapping at the ball during impact, you have used your wrists incorrectly. Although the power assembly accelerates when it begins the downswing, the golf swing's overall tempo should remain the same.

rhythms exists in the golf swing. Every time you swing the golf club, whether the action is simple or complex, your body is playing a rhythm. When you have hit the ball well, your body tries to repeat this rhythm. The rhythm may assume a different tempo. However, the body is always looking to work in harmony, so the basic beat remains the same.

Some swings rely solely on a tempo for their execution. This is why sometimes strange-looking swings produce positive results. The only problem with these swings is that if the tempo is off, there are no mechanics on which to fall back. As I have stated, sound mechanics create good timing; even when the body's timing is slightly off, the golfer will still manage to score a reasonable round of golf. This is why you do not see professional golfers shoot 72 one day and 95 the next. Their mechanics are sound enough to produce a consistent tempo that gets them consistently back to the ball.

We have seen the importance of the change of direction and its importance as a link between the backswing and the downswing. Once the change of direction has occurred, technically speaking, we have begun our downswing.

6

The Power Downswing

The downswing should be a reversal of the backswing. Once you have made a smooth change of direction, your body is set in motion. The downswing is the final, most crucial part of the golf swing. It is possible to make mistakes on the backswing and even the change of direction and still manage to deliver a direct hit to the ball. The downswing provides the last chance for these corrections to be made. Keep in mind that we are trying to create a repetitive swing, so in this case, that means swinging the club back to the ball, with as few compensations as possible. One of the most important power factors discussed in chapter 1 will now come into play—the club's downswing plane (swing path).

The Path to Power

Ideally, we want the club to follow a square swing path (in relation to the target) back to the ball. This is the most direct route to the ball, and as such it enables the arms to swing at their maximum speed. Being on the correct swing path helps our other power factors (see chapter 1) perform their roles and enables the club face to meet the ball squarely, with the club face pointing in our target's direction. It also helps to promote lag pressure (the cocked angle formed by the wrists). And because of our swing's angle of descent, it will ensure that maximum club-head speed is delivered to the ball.

POWER TIP
The correct downswing path is usually defined as an inside-to-outside swing plane. Many professionals teach golfers to intentionally try to swing from the inside to the outside on the downswing. This is incorrect and often leads to pushed shots (shots that go to the right). If you simply allow your arms to return on the same, or close to the same, plane as your backswing, you will go from inside to outside.

Swing planes often alter during a golf swing. The backswing plane is not always the same as the downswing plane. This shifting on the downswing is usually influenced by the part of the body that initiates the downswing. So it is not uncommon for a golfer to swing back to the ball on a plane that takes a slightly outside or inside path to the ball. Sometimes this path will even shift to the outside on the downswing and still remain on an inside path in relation to the target line.

The Downswing Path and Ball Spin

The downswing path will affect what type of spin will be imparted to the golf ball. This spin, in turn, will be a determining factor in the distance the ball will travel. On a tee shot, have you ever seen a ball take a high trajectory and then land with very little roll? In this situation we would say that the ball had a large amount of backspin, which means that the manner in which the ball was struck gave it forward momentum and a backward spinning motion. If you have any knowledge of billiards, you will understand how this occurs. When you want the cue ball to stop or move backward after it contacts the targeted ball, you aim at the bottom half of the cue ball. The cue ball moves forward with backspin that, upon contact, will move the ball backward or cause it to stop. If you want the cue ball to roll after contact, you aim toward the top part of the ball, giving the ball forward spin and momentum, which, upon contact, will cause it to keep rolling. In golf, during the tee shot, if the ball is struck by the driver with a descending blow, backspin—which usually results in a loss of power—will occur. If the ball is struck with an ascending blow, a topspin—which will result in greater roll—results. A side spin is created when the club face glances across the ball. Side spin can control the ball's direction and result in a significant loss of power. Perhaps the most dreaded shot produced by side spin is the slice (see page 66). With a slice the ball begins on a straight trajectory, then veers sharply toward the right, easily resulting in a loss of 15–20 yards. One can see that ball spin is extremely important in a power swing.

The Path of Least Resistance

The ideal downswing plane is a circular path on a plane which was established at the address. This is the path of least resistance for the power angle. Experiment for yourself. Swing the golf club to the top of your backswing. Now swing the club on an outside-to-inside path. Try taking this path in slow motion. Notice the steep incline at which you approach the ball. This type of descent forces you to lose your power angle and, consequently, to cast your club. This is the path most golfers take on their downswing. The club's sharp descent and subsequent uncocking of the wrists create a hacking or chopping sensation; hence, the expressions "I'm hacking at the ball" or "I feel like I'm chopping wood." The club face's position at contact will determine the direction and power of the resulting shot.

An inside downswing path is usually more desired than an outside path. Again, experiment for yourself. Notice that when the club is on an inside path, it is easier to maintain your power angle. The reason for this is that the angle of descent is not as steep; therefore, it is easier for the weighted club head to lag behind the hands.

The Power Assembly on the Downswing

We have seen the importance of keeping your power assembly intact during the change of direction. However, at some point, that assembly will come undone to meet the golf ball. First let me emphasize that the disassembly of the power assembly is not a conscious, contrived motion; rather, it should occur by inertial effects. The arms and hands simply facilitate this disassembly and the consequent follow-through. The power assembly will begin to disassemble when the club face begins to square to the ball (see Figs. 33 and 34). It is at this point that the right elbow will begin to straighten and the wrists will start uncocking. This all occurs in a split second, so there is no conscious method of controlling the disassembly. The best we can do is understand this disassembly and train our arms, hands, and body to facilitate, not hinder, the swinging club.

POWER TIP
Never intentionally force your right elbow toward your hip on the downswing. Simply allow the power assembly to return on the arc created by the backswing.

The Hands on the Downswing

On the downswing the hands should work together. This can be a very difficult accomplishment for many players. It is only natural for your dominant hand to try to take control on the downswing. As we have seen, our power angle should remain intact during the start of the downswing. To do this, both hands must be

FIGURE 33. As the power center turns and the club face begins to point toward the ball, the wrists will begin to straighten.

FIGURE 34. At impact the wrists will have straightened and the right elbow will remain slightly bent. Immediately after impact the elbow will straighten.

POWER TIP

Trying to make the butt of the club point toward the ball on the downswing is a frequently used exercise to teach golfers to maintain the power angle on the downswing. But this can be a very damaging exercise which actually teaches golfers to shank the ball. For the beginning-to-advanced golfer, never intentionally maintain the power angle for more than a foot on your downswing.

moving with equal momentum. The problem most golfers discover (assuming that they are right-handed) is that the mere sight of the golf ball elicits a hitting response from the right hand—a very natural desire. You have an object you want to hit, and you want to hit it with power. It is natural for the right hand (or left hand in the case of the left-handed golfer) to try to take control. This hitting action, when it occurs, causes a casting motion, and the power angle is lost. The hands should always lead the club head until after impact. At that point, they will move with the club head until the wrists cock, as they did on the backswing; only this time they will cock on the follow-through (see chapter 7).

The Hand Release

I believe that the release of the hands at impact is probably the most misunderstood part of the golf swing. The hands do not release by flipping; rather, they straighten and act as a swivel. The release is the point at which the hands change directions, when the back of the left hand no longer points to right of, but rather down, the target line. Many golfers believe that this release is intentional, while others believe that you should never think about your hands on the downswing; it happens naturally. Both are incorrect. It is impossible at the moment when the ball is struck to make your hands release. The swing is moving too quickly. If you attempt to do this, you will end up losing acceleration, and again you have lost your power angle. Additionally, it is quite important to understand and practice the hand's proper role in the hitting area.

Let's analyze the release by swinging the club with one hand at a time, starting with the left. Swing the club to the top of your backswing. Now let it swing through. Allow the toe of the club to point toward the sky on the backswing and then again on the follow-through. You will notice that the club face is following the upper body's rotation. At the address, the power center points to the right of the target line; the club face, toward the target (see Fig. 35). Halfway on the backswing, the club face points to the right of the target line, while the power center is turned 45 degrees to the right. When you swing back toward the ball, the power center points to the right of the target line, and the club face points toward the target (the same as in the address position). Halfway on the follow-through the power center is pointing toward the target, and the club face is pointing left of the target line. In other words, the power center is dictating in which direction the hands and the club face. The wrists and arms are not releasing or acting independently. The release is the point

POWER TIP
Women are often told to snap their wrists at impact. This is usually a very destructive concept, for when you do so, your hands are decelerating, and the club head is out of control.

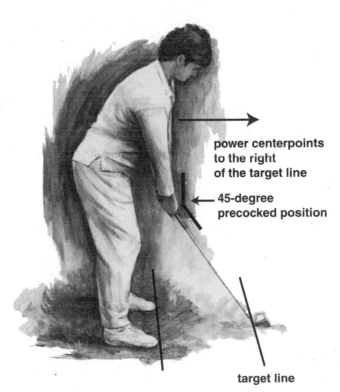

power centerpoints
to the right
of the target line

45-degree
precocked position

target line

FIGURE 35.

at which the power center moves from pointing to the right side to pointing toward the left side, and the neutral position between the two is the impact position. Thus, it wasn't wrist action that created the club head's release; it was the upper body's rotation that dictated the point of transition or the hand's release. Notice on the backswing how the wrists are cocked and how, by the time you reach impact, they straighten. How did they get into the straight position without uncocking?

At the address, our wrists are in a precocked position (refer again to Fig. 35). Already our power angle has been formed, because the wrists are at a 45-degree angle with the arms. At the top of your backswing your wrists are cocked at a 90-degree angle. On the downswing this angle is maintained. Many golfers believe that the wrist release is the flipping of the hands at impact. The release actually involves two motions on the downswing. There is an uncocking motion, where the wrists straighten, and there is a swiveling motion. Both these motions are related to the power center's rotation.

At the top of your backswing the palm of your right hand faces right of your target line, and your wrists are fully cocked. Your wrist will maintain this cocked position as long as your palm faces right. However, at the point when the arms swing along with the rotating power center and the palm of the right hand begins to point toward the ball, there is a downward flexion (uncocking) of the wrist caused by the weight of the club head and the straightening of the right elbow (see Fig. 35). As the hand squares to the ball and follows the power center to the left of the target line, there is a torque, or swiveling motion (see Fig. 36). This type of release is created by the wrists uncocking 90 degrees and the swiveling flexion of the wrist bone as the hands follow the power center. The back of the right wrist remains supinated throughout the swing. The wrist bone should never flex so that the back of the right wrist is pronated (see Fig. 37).

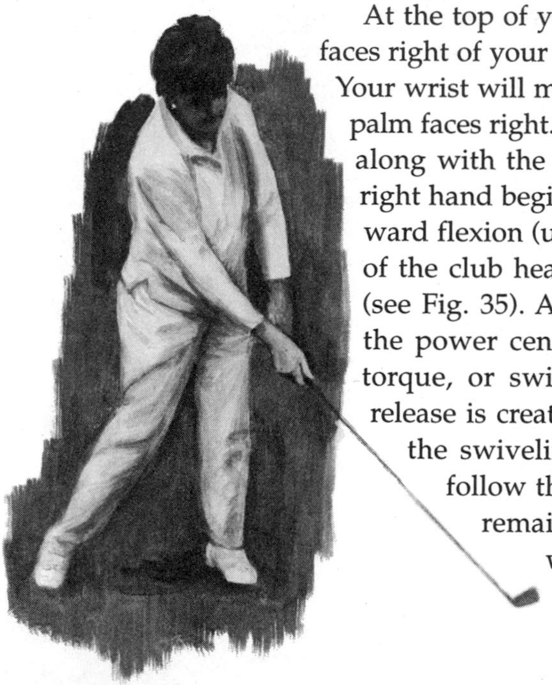

Lag Pressure and the Release

FIGURE 36. Notice how the right hand faces in the direction opposite that of the downswing.

We have seen how the power angle on the downswing creates club-head lag, meaning, as the name suggests, that the club head is lagging behind the hands on the downswing. As the club head lags behind the hands on the downswing, it will build up kinetic energy, which we have described as lag pressure. As the hands are swinging on an arc, the club head will lag behind the hands, with little pressure from the weight of the club head to undo the power angle. As the club swings on this radial arc, it is building radial lag pressure (which is power in a kinetic form). The faster the hands move, the more lag pressure created. When the club starts to swing down the target line, the weight of the club head, coupled with its speed, forces the hands to release their lag pressure in the form of a pure energy. This is the release and should occur at the impact area. This is the optimum speed of the club head during the golf swing.

FIGURE 37. The right wrist bone is pronated: an exaggeration of the scoop release.

Releasing the Hands Prematurely

We have just seen what constitutes a proper release and the importance of maintaining the power assembly on the downswing. Now let us discuss what occurs when the wrists release improperly. It is extremely important that the avid female golfer, seeking to improve her game, understand the theory and pitfalls of an early wrist release. The reason I single out women is that a man's upper-body strength enables him to employ an incorrect release and still get distance. This distance, of course, is not acquired through technique but through pure brute force. When a woman employs an early release, she is severely punished with loss of distance. So you can see how it is crucial that a woman understand this part of the swing.

The most common problem on the downswing regarding the wrists is casting (see Fig. 5), called such because the wrists literally cast the club head as if it were a fishing rod. In this process, the power angle will be lost, and no lag pressure will be created. The wrists, when casting the club head, will affect our other power factors (see chapter 1). This casting motion will also affect our downswing plane, the angle of descent, the impact area of the club face, and the club head's speed. One can see that our power angle is quite important to our distance. Equally

POWER TIP
Swinging of the club on an inside-to-outside downswing path enables radial lag pressure to build. With a steep outside-to-inside downswing plane, it is harder to maintain the power angle; consequently, you will lose lag pressure.

important is the point in the golf swing that the loss of the power angle occurs. For example, if this uncocking is the first move on your downswing, it will have a more dramatic effect than when the uncocking occurs at hip height. As you will recall from chapter 5, the power assembly will remain intact until about the time the power center points to the right of the target line and the palm of the right hand begins to face down the target line. At this point the wrists will perform two motions: a downward flexion and a swivel or torque. Thus, the wrists will naturally begin to straighten at about the hip level. Consequently, a casting motion here will not have as severe an effect as it did at the top of the backswing.

However, there is another type of early wrist release that often occurs at about hip level that is as harmful as the loss of the power angle at the top of the backswing. This is a scoop release. A scoop release occurs when the back of the right wrist straightens and eventually pronates at impact (see Fig. 37). It affects the same power factors as our casting motion. The scoop release is commonly used by golfers who have trouble getting the ball airborne, who try to help the ball into the air by scooping with the right wrist. If you have strong wrists (like many men), you can get some distance with this maneuver, but this type of release hampers power in many women's swings. You can tell if you have used the scoop release by the wrist's position at the finish: If the right wrist bone is pronated, chances are you have tried to scoop the ball into the air.

Connectivity

The hand release distinguishes whether a golf swing employed a hitting motion or a swinging motion. A hitting motion usually requires more strength (in the forearms and hands). A swinging motion relies more on a whipping effect that forces the arms to swing at a high rate of speed. But it is not all black and white. A golfer can apply a combination of both methods to hit the ball.

The distinction between the two methods depends on how much forearm and wrist action is involved on the downswing's impact. For example, if on your downswing your hand movement closely follows your power center's rotation, you are probably a hitter. With a hitter, the straightening of the right elbow and wrist on the downswing and the right side itself is the source of power. With a swinger, the speed of the swinging arms moves so that they are less connected with the power center. A result of this is greater wrist and forearm rotation. This forearm and hand rotation is fine to a degree, but the more the rotation, the less connected the arms and hands are to the power center. This lack of coordination with the power center's movement equals a loss of accuracy and power (see chapter 14 for the "stay connected" drill).

Your body's build can also influence your swing type. If your shoulders are wide and your arms muscular and short, you probably tend toward a hitting motion. However, if you are tall, with long arms, you'll have a tendency toward wrist rotation, which would make you more inclined to produce a swinging motion. Because of a woman's flexibility and the torque created by the hips, most women are considered swingers.

This discussion of swingers and hitters reminds me of an instance when I said to a slightly elderly woman, "From the move on your downswing I would think you're a swinger." She looked at her husband, who was just an ear's length away, then turned back to me, winked, and said proudly, "No one has called me that in years!"

POWER TIP

A popular swing theory of the past was that of forearm rotation. This means rotating the forearms on the backswing and then back through on the downswing. The theory supposedly boasted an increase in distance because of the additional rotation. But this forearm rotation (unless your forearms are extremely strong) really only results in a loss of power because of the loss of connectivity.

A Strong Release

The strength of the release should be relative to the upper body's (the power center's) rotational speed. That a golfer has a strong release at impact tells us that her arms and hands are moving quickly. Remember, the point of release occurs when the power center moves from a neutral position to point toward the target. Of course, the arms and hands should be following this path. Consequently, the faster the center travels, the faster the hands will release. The more detached the forearms and wrists are from the center's movement during the release, the less club-head speed will be generated. One example is when you intentionally try to force the release or the speed of the release (see Fig. 38).

FIGURE 38. The hands are forcing rather than swinging with the club head.

POWER TIP

To release the club correctly, your hands need to be trained in their proper role. When the hands know their function, we say they are educated. The best way to educate the hands is through drills. I strongly advise reviewing the section in chapter 14 for wrist-release exercises.

Tempo and the Casting Motion

Casting is particularly difficult to cure because it becomes intertwined with one's tempo. Recall the chapter on tempo and timing and the chapter on the change of direction. We have seen how the change of direction is the critical time for most swings. It is at this point that the "and" in the "one," "two," "and" "three" represents the change of direction. When the downswing is initiated by a casting motion, your tempo becomes more of a "one," "two," "and" "a" "three." Once this tempo is established, your body's internal sense of rhythm incorporates this extra "a" as part of its natural tempo. When this happens, it is very difficult to change this casting without throwing off your internal sense of rhythm. So keep in mind that when you are working on maintaining your power assembly on the downswing, times can get difficult on the course, increasing the possibility for a few high scores.

Grip Pressure Points on the Downswing

Placing the heel of your left hand on top of the club's shaft helps to produce, but does not guarantee, a viselike effect on the downswing. If the pressure points in the right hand are not correct, then even the viselike grip position of the left hand will be to no avail. At the top of the backswing, it is not unusual for an amateur golfer's grip pressure to change. This change in pressure from the original address grip can force a golfer to lose her power angle. It is important to be aware of your downswing's pressure points; if you are not, you could be destroying your power assembly's ability to create club-head speed.

Your first inclination on the downswing is probably to uncock your wrists to deliver the club head to the ball. When this is done, pressure is generated by the left and right thumbs and the right forefinger. This is simply a reaction to a stimulus; in other words, your subconscious tries to implement the fastest possible method of delivering the club head to the ball. There are several different pressure points that can be applied in combination to facilitate the maintenance of the power angle. One is pressure from the left hand's heel, with little pressure from the right hand's thumb or thumb's pad. With the second and third fingers of the right hand, the right forefinger will act like a talon, applying ample backward and downward pressure, respectively, that locks the club into its power position. This pressure with the forefinger usually forces the right thumb's pad to deliver very little pressure. When this is the case, it is not unusual at the top of the backswing for the right thumb's pad to barely touch the thumb of the left hand.

Another combination of grip pressures on the downswing is for the first two fingers of the left hand and the thumb's pad of the right to apply pressure on the downswing. When this combination of pressure points is applied, it is not unusual for the butt of the club to separate slightly from the left hand's heel on the downswing. The pressure from the right thumb's pad forces the left arm into a straighter downswing position and keeps the power angle in formation on the downswing. The different combinations of pressure points will depend on the size and strength of your hands and whether you are a hitter or a swinger. Most importantly, we do not want to create any type of grip pressure on the downswing that promotes the uncocking of our power angle.

Power Anchors on the Downswing

The Hips

In chapter 3 we discussed our power anchors. Now let's see what role they play on the downswing. The primary power anchors on the downswing are the hips. Women's hip movement in the golf swing usually receives a great deal of attention, mainly because women usually have more to move in the hip department than men! However, this movement should not be viewed as a source of power. Rather, the hips should provide a lower center of gravity which will provide stability as the upper body unwinds. The well-anchored, 45-degree turn by the hips, compared to the 90-degree turn by the shoulders, will create torque between the upper and lower body.

We have seen how the first move on the downswing is the upper body's arms and hands returning on the same, or approximate, downswing path. As the arms move upon this arc, the hips will respond by moving out of the way. This slight movement of the hips creates an uncoiling effect, which helps to enhance the power center's rotational speed. The idea is that the upper body is trying to catch up to the lower body. The closer the upper body comes to catching the hips, the more power generated. The farther the hips get in front of the upper body (leave the upper body behind), the greater the chances for an errant

POWER TIP
Do not try to create power by using your hips. Misuse of the hips is the most common cause of errant tee shots and loss of power.

shot and subsequent loss of power. It is the power center's rotational speed, not the hips, that generates power.

Hip Rotation

Not only are the hips often improperly perceived as a direct source of power for a golf swing; their actual downswing motion is also often misinterpreted. Perhaps one of the most misleading and commonly used phrases in golf is "hip rotation."

The hips do not only rotate. The rotation is combined with a lateral movement. The first movement the hips make is a lateral and rotating motion. These two motions begin with the lateral move being the greater. It is only after the power center squares up to the ball that the rotation of the hips is greater than their lateral movement. Keep in mind that the power center tries to catch the hips on the downswing but never quite does until the finish.

The Legs and Feet

During the downswing, your weight should shift from the top of the backswing position, where most of the weight is on the right foot, to the follow-through position, where all the weight is on the left foot. Remember, the legs and feet provide a base on which the upper body rotates. As such, it is very important that they respond to your upper body's movement on the backswing as well as the downswing. Many times women are told that the first movement necessary for creating power on the downswing is the weight shifting from the right to left foot. In one sense, this is correct, because the weight shifts in response to the upper body uncoiling and the arms' and hands' forward motion. However, the legs should not be used as a cue to initiate the downswing (unless, of course, your legs are slow to respond and need some impetus). The golf swing is a motion that moves from the right to the left. As your body unwinds on the downswing, it should be instinctive for the shifting of this weight to occur.

When viewing pictures of famous golfers, you will notice that their heads are behind the ball at the moment of impact. However, you must realize that the head is in this position for a split second and will be forced forward toward the target by momentum. You never want to try to emulate this position, for two reasons. First, when you intentionally try to keep the head still, it will usually stay in that position for more than a split second. Because of this, the head will not release properly, and a bad shot will result. Second, the professional golfer is not forcing her head into this position. It is simply the result of a good downswing path.

When the club takes an outside-to-inside downswing path, the right shoulder will move outside its ideal path. When the right shoulder moves in such a manner, it will force the head to move forward. The amount of this movement depends on the severity of the downswing path. However, when the club's downswing path is on or slightly inside the backswing's path, the right shoulder does not come out and around. Consequently, the head will remain behind the ball longer than with the outside-to-inside path. Again, the head simply responds to the swing's movement; it should not dictate it.

The Power Position at Impact

One common element of all great golfers is their impact position (see Figs. 39 and 36). The most important element at impact is the hand's relationship to the club head and the position of the wrists. You will notice from the illustration that at impact the back of the right wrist is convex, while the back of the left wrist is straight. Another important part of the impact position is that the wrists are now straight, and the upper body's power center is pointing in the direction of the ball. The weight is shifting toward the left foot. Remember to keep in mind that this is a picture of the impact position. It depicts a fraction of a second of a swinging motion. Do not try to force yourself into this position at impact; doing so will cause nothing but trouble. Be aware that this ideal impact position is accomplished only through a correct swinging motion.

The Power Center on the Downswing

Remember, the power center is the motor of the golf swing. Once you have made the change of direction, this center is in motion. The arms and hands will be swinging, trying to catch this center. They come close to this at impact, but the center should always be moving slightly ahead of the power assembly. Turning the power center on the downswing should never be a conscious effort. If you simply allow your arms and hands to

FIGURE 39. The impact position. Notice how the wrists have straightened.

return on the same or similar arc as the backswing, this center will move naturally. The center must move out of the way if the arms are to return on this arc.

Shots Resulting From an Outside-to-Inside Downswing Path

The Slice

Probably the most familiar term in golf is the word slice. The slice is the most common result of all errant tee shots. A slice's trajectory begins straight and then veers sharply toward the right. It is commonly called a banana ball. Slicing the ball results in a major loss of distance, not to mention accuracy. A slice occurs when the club head travels on an outside-to-inside downswing plane and the club face is pointed toward the target or slightly open (right of the target line). We have seen how an outside-to-inside swing plane produces a descending blow to the ball and how this creates backspin. The slice combines two spins: a backspin and a left-to-right side spin. The result is that the ball begins fairly straight because of its catapulting force; however, as the forward momentum diminishes, the side spin takes over, which results in a serious loss of yards (and often loss of golf balls if there are woods around). The amount of club-head speed you generate will determine how much distance you will lose during a sliced shot.

This leads to a question that I am frequently asked by men, which is: Why do women hit the ball so straight? I don't know how often I have heard: "Boy, if I had my wife's accuracy off the tee, my handicap would drop ten strokes." One reason why men don't hit the ball as straight as women is that men tend to use their hands and forearms incorrectly, which delivers the club face to the ball at an awkward angle. But in fairness to male golfers, it is not that women hit the ball that much straighter. It is that women usually generate less club-head speed, which, in turn, imparts less spin. Let me give you an example: On the downswing, if the club face is pointing toward the target and its swing path has been outside to inside, a slice will result. If you replicate this motion by swinging your arms very slowly, you'll notice that the ball moves slightly to the right. However, the faster you let your arms swing and the more club-head speed you generate, the more you will see the ball slice. It's simple physics: The more power imparted to the ball, the greater the spin, and thus a more dramatic slice.

For many golfers the slice is the most dreaded tee shot. It is estimated that 90 percent of all golfers slice the ball. Besides the loss of distance, this shot is feared because golf courses are designed to punish the right-handed slicer. (The reason I have noted right-handed golfers is that a left-handed golfer's slice will move in the opposite direction [right to left] of the right-handed golfer.) Take note of where the hazards on your golf course are located. For a tee shot they are often situated toward the right side of the fairway, just about the distance of an average drive.

The Pulled Slice

A pulled slice simply means that instead of the ball starting on a straight path toward your target, it begins left of the target, then veers sharply to the right. This usually occurs because your downswing is on a very strong outside-to-inside plane. In other words, your downswing plane is way left of your target, but your club face is open. The forward momentum will then take the ball to the left, and when the momentum diminishes, the side spin will take over, making the ball veer sharply to the right. The one positive aspect of a pulled slice is that since the ball starts to the left, when it slices, it often manages to land on the right edge of the fairway. This is a difficult way to play golf (constantly flirting with disaster), yet many high handicappers, although not willingly, subscribe to this shot.

The Pulled Hook

Very few golfers really hook the ball. Instead, most pull-hook the ball. Although the results in either case are not good, a pulled hook differs from a regular hook in two ways. A pulled hook will begin either dead left or just slightly left of the target and then veer strongly to the left. This occurs because the swing path is outside to inside, with the club face slightly closed (pointing to the left at impact). A true hook is created by an inside-to-outside swing path, and the ball usually will start on a path directly toward or slightly to the right of the target. Ninety-five percent of all hooks are pulled hooks. A pulled hook is actually very similar to a slice, with the only difference being the direction in which the club face is pointing at the moment of impact.

The Pulled Shot

Your regular pulled shot is just as it sounds: it is a shot pulled to the left as your arms pull across your body. This shot starts left and continues to travel in a straight line left of your target. With a pulled shot the club face and swing path are square to one another, but the problem is that they are both pointing toward the left. The good thing about a pulled shot is that you will usually hit the daylights out of the ball if it is pulled. As the arms swing across the body, they generate better leverage and more force; hence, better club-head speed. This increase in distance also occurs because you are not delivering as sharp a descending blow to the ball. Since your swing plane and club face are pointing in the same direction, the club will not take too steep a descent toward the ball. The bad news is that the ball will be going in the wrong direction.

You might notice that right and left shots are really caused by the same two factors: the direction the club face is pointing at impact and the club's downswing path. Remember that the slice was caused by the club swinging down across the ball (outside to inside), with the club face pointing toward the target. Now, if you take that same swing, only this time at impact the club face points toward the left, you will have a pulled shot. So, with one minor adjustment (closing the club face), the same swing that hit the ball to the right can cause the ball to go to the left. A slice and a pull are really a product of the same motion.

The Fade

There are varying degrees of outside-to-inside motion and, vice versa, inside-to-outside motion. Coming over the top, outside-to-inside, is not as terrible as you have been taught to think. Often, coming from too far inside your target line on the downswing can be much more devastating. The two shots created by a slight outside to inside and inside to outside on the downswing are the fade and the draw (see page 70 for the draw). A fade is a shot in which the ball moves slightly from the right to the left. Instead of veering to the right like a slice, a fade starts slightly left of the target and then drops gently to the right. The fade has always had the reputation of being a very controlled shot. Since the ball has a slight descending blow when hitting an approach shot to the green, the ball will stop nicely on the green with backspin.

Shots Resulting From an Inside-to-Outside Downswing Path

One thing to remember when dealing with an inside-to-outside downswing path is that you are delivering an ascending blow to the ball. We have seen how a descending blow can impart backspin. Well, an ascending blow will do the opposite; it will impart topspin. A topspin usually results in more roll and greater distance. However, if too great a topspin is imparted to the ball, the result will be a topped shot, meaning that the top half of the ball has been hit. With this shot you will get plenty of roll, but unfortunately that is all you will get. A topped shot does not have much carry; it literally rolls on the ground (see Fig. 3C).

The Hook

It is said that all great golfers at one point in time have had a problem with hooking the ball. I have played golf with many aspiring players who took solace in this credo, particularly as they watched their ball veer sharply to the left and roll out of bounds. Fighting a hook is a terrible feeling. You are always afraid to really let loose on the ball because you live in constant fear of the ball hooking into the woods or water. The good news about hooking the ball, however, is that to produce such a shot, your downswing plane (the club path) is either correct or close to being correct. With a little work, a hook can always be controlled. However, as with a slice, the basic swing fundamentals are flawed in a hook, and it is therefore generally much harder to cure.

A hook usually occurs when the club travels on a path that is inside that of a square downswing path. It can also occur when the club takes the correct downswing path, but for some reason, the club face closes slightly at impact, which imparts a right-to-left side spin. A push and hook are created from the same inside-to-outside downswing plane. However, on a pushed shot, the club will travel on a more severe inside-to-outside path, and the club will point to the right of the target at impact.

The Pushed Shot

A pushed shot occurs when the ball starts and remains on a path that is to the right of its target. It is created when the club takes an inside-to-outside downswing path (to the right of your target

POWER TIP

If you have a chronic problem with the pushed shot, chances are the cause is incorrect hip rotation on the downswing. This incorrect rotation is called spinning out. The hips turn so quickly on the downswing that the club face is forced to the open position at impact and a pushed shot results. A good cure for this problem is to perform the hip-rotation exercise found in chapter 14.

line), with the club face also pointing toward the right (open). A pushed shot is nothing but trouble, particularly because most of the trouble on golf courses is on the right side of the fairway.

The Draw

A true draw has a very beautiful ball flight and is wonderful to watch. Many people believe that with a draw you aim to your right and plan for the ball to land 5–10 feet left of your target area. A draw can be accomplished in this manner, but it won't be a true draw. With a true draw, your club face is pointing straight at the target at your setup. When you hit the ball, it starts right of its target, then gently turns to the left and lands right on line. You can also put a nice backspin on a ball that draws. However, there is a smaller margin for error in doing this, so often a fade is preferred, particularly on approach shots. This is created from our inside-to-outside downswing path. So you can see how the ball might start to the right and then how the natural closing of the club face on the follow-through puts just a touch of spin on the ball and makes it turn back into the left and right on the target line.

The Duck Hook

The duck hook is also called a snap hook because the ball's flight literally snaps to the left. A duck hook usually occurs on tee shots. Not only does the ball snap to the left, but since the ball has a tremendous amount of topspin, it will also travel very close to the ground. When you hit this shot, you can be fairly assured of a lost ball, for when it hits the ground, it will roll forever!

We have now seen the different spins that can be imparted to the ball. You would think that after we had hit the ball, the rest of the golf swing would be inconsequential. In the following chapter we will find this is really not so.

POWER TIP
Because women have been taught to use their hips incorrectly on the downswing, many have a problem with their shots alternating from the left to the right. To use the hips correctly, read the section on "Power Anchors" in chapter 3.

7

The Power Finish

The follow-through, or finish, refers to the swing's motion after the ball has been struck. Although follow-through and finish are often used interchangeably, the finish can also literally mean when the swing is completed (see Figs. 40 and 41). A good follow-through should be the result of a good swing. Trying to emulate a correct finish usually does not work. The finish should just happen.

FIGURE 40. Front view of the finish.

FIGURE 41. A side view of the follow-through. Notice how the body is tilted at the same angle as at the address.

The follow-through tells us much about what has occurred on the downswing. For example, the position of the wrists and arms indicate the club's downswing path and whether we have cast the club head. By our weight's distribution, we can determine whether there was a problem on the backswings or downswings. Another good indicator is our power center. By its finish position we can often gauge the direction the ball has traveled and our club's downswing path. Thus, one can see that the follow-through is a good indicator of what has happened during the swing. However, there are certain fundamentals to be adhered to concerning the follow-through that will affect your downswing's ability to maintain its acceleration. Without these fundamentals, your downswing will be forced to decelerate; consequently, you will lose distance.

On a good downswing the club is accelerating. Anytime you lose acceleration in the golf swing, you can be almost certain that it will result in a casting motion. So the follow-through must give the downswing the ability to accelerate through the shot. Whenever you attempt to mimic a good follow-through (or perhaps the finish of your favorite professional golfer), your follow-through will become a contrived motion, not the result of a swinging motion. When this occurs, deceleration will result. The object is not to emulate a finish but to facilitate the downswing motion.

During the golf swing it is very important to maintain the same spine angle as at the address (to stay in one's posture). The only time you should come out of your posture is after you have hit the ball, completed your follow-through, and are looking to see where the ball has traveled. This notion of posture is especially important during the follow-through. The follow-through and the striking area are separated by nanoseconds. If you do pull out of your posture on your follow-through, chances are that this motion began in the hitting area.

Your wrists should be the first to break after your arms have fully extended from your body. This is essential for maintaining your posture. Once your arms are fully extended and your weight has been pulled completely toward your left side, the club must travel upward, in much the same manner as with the backswing. The wrists will be first to take the initial shock of the club returning toward the body. Immediately after the wrists have broken, the arms will begin to fold at the elbows.

The most common error made by women on the follow-through is that their arms and wrists fold too late. When this

POWER TIP

If you feel your torso lift up out of its posture on the finish, chances are that your wrists and elbows are breaking too late on the follow-through. Once your arms have fully extended from your body and toward the target, let the wrists and elbows bring the club back toward your body.

happens, the body is pulled up out of its posture, and the arms flail high into the air. The result is a loss of control over the club; this loss is usually accompanied by a finish where the club slaps against the golfer's back. It may look dramatic, and even appear powerful, but this is not the case.

Try this exercise, which involves maintaining your address posture through the hitting area. Take a club and put it in your right hand. Swing the club to the top of your backswing and let it swing through. On the follow-through, allow the wrist to cock the same as it did on the backswing. Notice how easy it is to stay in your posture. Now do the same exercise, only this time do not cock the wrist or permit much bend in the elbows on the follow-through. Notice how your arm gets pulled into the air and your right shoulder comes up and touches your chin. This motion will pull you up out of your posture on the follow-through.

Another factor is the direction the club face points after you hit the ball. The follow-through is basically a reversal of the backswing, so ideally the club face will point in the opposite direction of the backswing. For example, if, on your backswing, the club face points to the right of the target line, with the front of the club's toe pointing toward the sky, the club face will point to the left of the target, with the toe of the club again pointing toward the sky on the follow-through. If this does not happen but the club face continues to point down the target line, the torso will be forced to lift out of its posture.

You might ask, "What is the difference how I finish if the ball has already been hit?" This may be true to a degree. However, if your body is anticipating a certain finish, it will adjust the downswing to complete that finish. An incorrect finish (meaning it impedes the downswing's acceleration) will result in a loss of acceleration. One example is our wrists and arms folding too late on the follow-through. When the subconscious expects the arms to remain straight (rather than the wrists breaking), in order to bring the club back in toward the body, it will force the swing to decelerate. However, if the subconscious knows that the wrists will do the work, it can continue its acceleration on the follow-through. Any movement on the downswing that forces the body out of its posture at impact will cause deceleration. After you have hit the ball and your arms reach their full extension, your weight should be pulled completely onto your left foot. When this happens, your spine should straighten, but the shoulders should remain somewhat on their same tilt.

POWER TIP
Never try to stay behind the ball at impact. This will force you to finish with your back slightly arched and can cause back problems. Always allow your spine to straighten and your head to move to the left.

POWER TIP
*Your left elbow
sticking out at your
finish (chicken wing)
often indicates a
severe outside-to-
inside downswing
path.*

POWER TIP
*When the arms have
reached their full
extension on the
follow-through, it is
very important that
either the wrists cock
or that the elbows
fold 90 degrees;
otherwise, you will be
pulled out of your
posture.*

POWER TIP
*If, at your finish,
your right wrist bone
is pronated, your
release was incorrect.
The right wrist
should remain
supinated, the same
as at the address and
top of the backswing.*

POWER TIP
*"Finish high and let
it fly" is an idea that
many women try to
incorporate into their
swings. This may
"look good," but its
effects can be
disastrous unless the
finish is a result of
the downswing.*

The Head

When you finish your swing, you should be looking at your target, not at the ground. You should never be able to see the club head make contact with the ball. If you do, something is wrong. When you swing, your arms are accelerating, and your momentum is such that they will pull your head through and over to your left side. The head should merely go along for the ride. When the head does not move on the follow-through, it's like hitting a brick wall. When all your momentum is trying to swing to your target and it hits a stationary point, a deceleration of the club head results.

The Arms and Wrists

At and after impact, the arms, hands, and club head should be moving together. If, at this point, you notice that the wrists are broken, casting has taken place. This assembly should move together until the arms have reached their farthest extension from the body; that is, when the hands are completely extended from the body and the weight is onto the left side. It is physically impossible at this point for hands to travel any farther without actually pulling the body forward and falling over. Once this point is reached, the wrists begin to cock and form their power angle, as they did on the backswing. Immediately after the wrists cock, the arms will begin to fold. Although the arms have begun to fold, the wrists are in complete control of the club.

The height of your finish will be based on your backswing plane. If your backswing was upright, your finish will be upright. Conversely, golfers with flat backswing planes will tend to finish their swings on a flat plane. Never try to manipulate the height of your follow-through without also changing your backswing.

The Hips as a Power Anchor on the Follow-through

After impact, the hips will simply continue on their course. Their momentum is such that there should be no way to either slow them down or speed them up. Remember, the hips act as an anchor; you do not want them dictating the motion of the upper and lower body. The hips' motion should never be a spinning motion; they are simply getting out of the way so that the arms do not lose their acceleration.

The Power Center and the Follow-through

From the address position, the power center should turn 90 degrees to the right and then return 180 degrees to the left. It is precisely this rotation that is at the heart of the swing's rotation. Ideally, at our finish, our power center should be facing our target. The position of this center can reveal problems with the backswing or downswing. For example, the center being pointed far left of the target's line can indicate many problems. Perhaps the shoulders never made a complete turn on the backswing, causing overrotation on the follow-through. Or the swing path was simply so severely outside to inside that the center was pulled to the left (a pulled shot). Another possibility may be that the hips have spun out (gotten far ahead of the torso), forcing the center to spin to the left.

When the center finishes pointing toward the right, you can be pretty certain the result will be a pushed shot (flies straight right). This is usually caused by an extremely inside path on the downswing. It also can be caused by trying to keep one's eyes on the ball at impact. When this happens, the center does not complete its rotation; rather, it points toward the right. Because the center stops, the arms and hands go whipping through at impact, which shuts down the club face. The result is often a snap hook.

And there are times when the center points straight toward the target with no overrotation or underrotation, and because the center has moved properly, all the weight has shifted to the left foot. The swing will have felt effortless, and you will feel so good, you'll want to hold your finish for an eternity. This, my friends, keeps us coming back for more.

The Feet

At your finish, your weight should be on your left side (see Fig. 42). Your right toe should be touching the ground, with your right heel in the air. However, there is an important distinction to make here. Your right foot should be on its toes because its heel has been pulled to the left. The right heel should

POWER TIP

Many golfers, particularly women, believe the adage that at your finish your belt buckle should point toward your target. This is fine if you complete your swing in this position. However, never intentionally try to force your hips to turn so that your belt buckle is pointing toward your target.

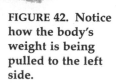

FIGURE 42. Notice how the body's weight is being pulled to the left side.

POWER TIP
Don't look at the ground after you hit the ball. If you do, your power center will not be able to rotate properly. Improper rotation will make you lose power and develop a chopping or hacking motion.

POWER TIP
Many women spring their right heel into the air on the follow-through. Be careful not to do this. Although it is your body's natural attempt to create power by leverage, it does not work in golf.

POWER TIP
You may see famous professionals swing where the left leg straightens and there is a lifting onto their toes at impact. Leave that swing to the professionals. What you are seeing is the result of a certain type of power swing. You do not want to emulate this. It will only get you into trouble.

not move up and to the left. If it does, there can be several causative factors. One is that the body has sprung upward at impact in an attempt to generate power. Another is that you have cast the club head with your wrists and your body is lifting in an attempt to keep the club from hitting the ground.

Weight Distribution at the Finish

Perhaps the best indicator of trouble in a golf swing is your weight distribution at the swing's finish. Whenever you fall backward after a shot, particularly on your drive, you know something went wrong. This backward movement is called a reverse pivot. It means that your weight was on the left side at the top of your backswing. Being in this position, it had nowhere to move except to the right on the follow-through; hence, the name reverse pivot. I'm not sure where the term pivot came from, for it really isn't a pivot. Consequently, many golf professionals call this motion a reverse weight shift. To me it is just a question of semantics, so I will often use the common, though incorrect, term reverse pivot. That you have fallen away from the ball has probably told you much about your swing. For example, if it is a reverse pivot, chances are that your shoulders turned incorrectly on the backswing, probably on too steep a plane (dipping under your chin). Thus, one can see how the finish is a good indicator of a fault in the backswing or down-swing motions.

You should now understand the importance of the follow-through. In order to finish in the wrong position, the club head has had to have decelerated at or before impact. This is why we must train our bodies in the correct follow-through motions, which will ensure club-head acceleration.

8

The Geometry
of the Golf Swing

The golf swing is comprised of an assortment of angles. These angles make the game of golf a game of technique. It is not so much the strength of a swing as it is its geometry. Without geometric symmetry, the golf swing is nothing but brute force. The wonderful part of golf's geometry is that anyone, despite their strength, can put its application to use. However, without the knowledge of these angles, weaker players will be left with a powerless swing.

The first angles we will concern ourselves with are those established at the address. At the end of chapter 3, we discussed how the body's angular relationship segmented the body, enabling body parts to function independently. These angles include the 45-degree angle created by the wrists and forearms and the 45-degree tilt of the upper body at the address.

Once we have created these address angles, our next concern is the creation of the power assembly. This is the 90-degree shoulder turn and wrist cock and depending on your arm length and backswing plane, the approximate 90-degree bend of your right elbow. Included in this power assembly is the spinal column's 45-degree tilt, the same angle (tilt) the spinal column assumed at the address. These angles will be anchored by the hips, and torque will be created by the difference between the 45-degree hip turn and the shoulder's 90-degree turn at the top of the backswing. Once these angles are established at the top of our backswing, the movement of these angles will be as relative and constant as possible. For example the 45-degree tilt by the upper body should remain as such through impact. The 90-degree shoulder turn will rotate 180 degrees to its finish position. This means that the shoulders turned 90 degrees on the backswing and, from the address position, 90 degrees on the follow-through. Thus, the amount of forward swing rotation is equal to the backswing rotation, and when combined, it gives you a total downswing and follow-through rotation of 180 degrees. The hips will rotate in somewhat the same manner, with total rotation on the downswing being approximately 135 degrees.

While your torso and lower body are moving, your power assembly, the 90-degree angles formed by the cocked wrists and the folded elbow, will maintain their relationship until the club face begins to point toward the ball. At this point, the 90-degree wrist cock and the right elbow will begin to straighten. On your follow-through, your wrists will again cock 90 degrees, and your body will remain in its 45-degree posture.

Let's leave the classroom and put geometry aside for a moment. The point of all these angles and degrees is that the golf swing involves technique and that all the muscle in the world is no substitute for good technique. So the next time you swing a club, realize that you have utilized the physics of about five different angles all working together. And you thought you were just swinging a club!

The Golf Swing as a Dynamic Event

Although the swing consists of many static positions, after the start of your swing these static positions turn into a dynamic event and should be in constant motion through to the finish. When explaining the golf swing, it is difficult to relate static positions to a dynamic motion. For example, we know that the power center at impact should be pointing in the vicinity of the ball. But we also have to realize that although it is pointing in this direction, it is also moving. So although you should be aware of the center's approximate positioning at impact, you cannot consciously place it in that position while swinging a club.

Another example is when a golfer consciously tries to square the back of her left hand toward her target at impact.

Again, this can be devastating for the golf swing. By squaring the left hand, you are trying to apply a static position to a dynamic event. Considering that the moment of impact lasts about 0.0005 seconds, such a feat is unlikely. In fact, when practiced regularly, this exercise will lead to a blocked shot. A blocked shot is one that travels to the right and is caused by the club face continuing to point down the target line well after impact. There is nothing wrong with rehearsing this concept while practicing; however, realize that this position must be integrated into the swing's general motion.

The geometry of golf may consist of many positions and angles, but you must realize that what we are trying to create is repetitive dynamic motion consisting of a multitude of approximate positions.

POWER TIP
Whenever you practice a drill that teaches a specific swing position, always make sure you finish your swing. For example, in an attempt to learn the hand's impact position, many golfers will practice stopping the club at impact. Golf is a dynamic motion. When practicing a static position, the resulting dynamic positions should be practiced as well. So if you are practicing your impact position, be sure on your last swing to complete your follow-through.

The Movement Toward One

All angles and body movement in the golf swing should culminate in unification at impact, not separate on the downswing.

On the backswing the hips turn 45 degrees; the shoulders, 90. The hands, which have the greatest distance to travel, will move on an approximate 112-degree arc into their backswing position. The idea on the downswing is not to separate these parts but to unite them. The power center tries to catch up to the hips, while the hands try to catch the power center, and last but certainly not least, the club head will make a mad dash to catch up to all the other parts. Because the golf swing is a dynamic motion, these parts briefly unite at impact but are always in motion until the finish. By uniting, I mean that the impact area will resemble the address position. You will notice that at impact the power center has caught up to the hips because they are in the same position as at the address (see Fig. 43). The hands have caught up to the

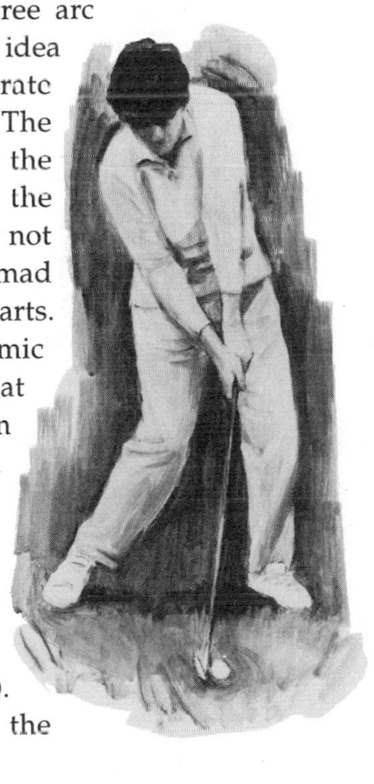

FIGURE 43. The hands lead the club head at impact.

POWER TIP

One constant in this dynamic event is the angle at which the upper body is tilted at the address. This posture, or tilt, should be maintained through the impact area and is appropriately described as staying in one's posture.

power center, and the club head has almost caught the hands. It is this final struggle toward unity, the golf swing's movement toward one, that creates power. The feeling of oneness at impact is both effortless and powerful. Movement away from this unity at any time means that one part of your body has jumped far ahead of the other. The result is wasted energy.

9

Misconceptions of Power

In the book's introduction, I stated that misinformation about the source of power in the golf swing is the greatest obstacle confronted by most women. This misinformation is sometimes given maliciously, from simple lack of concern or because the instructors themselves do not understand the correct power sources. Often these power tips can be gotten from a well-meaning golf partner or the most recent edition of your favorite golf magazine. Whatever the source, after reading this book, you should be able to begin to sort the good information from the bad. The following sections will address some of these common misconceptions. It is hoped that the information therein will save you time, effort, and a few strokes.

Incorrect Power Sources

Every golfer has at some point been told that she can generate more power by using a specific part of her anatomy. Unfortunately, this is usually incorrect information. If it were true that one part of your anatomy was responsible for power, you would then see golf professionals and amateurs alike constantly applying that part of their body to their golf swing. The problem is, there is not "one" part of the body that creates power. In fact, the more you try to utilize these incorrect power sources, the more likely you are to lose distance. Listed below are the most commonly taught misconceptions about acquiring power.

1. *The shoulders create power on the backswing. If you want to hit the ball farther, make more of a shoulder turn.* The truth of the matter is, a 90-degree shoulder turn is sufficient. More of a turn and you will have put your body out of balance, into a reverse pivot (see chapter 8).

2. *The hips are a major source of power.* The hips are not a direct source of power. However, by acting as a power anchor on the backswing, they create torque between the upper and lower body, which will be power producing on the downswing. Their uncoiling on the downswing is a reaction to the power center, and the arms and hands swinging back toward the ball (see chapter 6).

3. *You have to keep your left arm straight on the backswing.* The more rigid you keep your left arm on the backswing, the more it will be inclined to break down at the top of the backswing. It is the correct execution of the backswing through the proper wrist cock and grip that creates a straight left arm (see chapter 4).

4. *A strong leg drive is essential for power.* When the club swings back on an incorrect swing plane, a strong leg drive can put the club back onto a more powerful downswing plane (see chapter 6). However, this type of swing is unorthodox and not one I would recommend for a beginning-to-average golfer. On the downswing, the legs should respond to the arms and hands swinging back toward the ball. The lower body should respond to the upper body; it should not dictate the downswing.

5. *It is important to snap the wrists at the ball to generate power.* The wrists should never snap at the ball. The entire idea of the downswing is to let the wrists facilitate the club's motion. The wrists should never take control at impact by consciously forcing the club head. Once this is done, you will decelerate and consequently lose power. Because the downswing occurs in a split second, it is impossible to control the impact area by snapping the wrists. Educate the hands and wrists in their proper role by practicing their position after impact (see chapter 6).

6. *Tuck your right elbow into your side on the downswing.* This is often taught to create club-head lag pressure (ensure that the power assembly stays intact). If the power assembly stays intact,

it will give the appearance that the golfer is intentionally tucking her elbow in toward her side. Consequently, many golfers feel that if they consciously tuck their right elbows into their right sides, they can maintain their power assembly. Once the power assembly is set, it must move together on the downswing; in this movement the elbow is locked in a viselike position. You do not intentionally want to collapse your elbow in toward your body. The right elbow is the mechanism that keeps the left arm extended and the power assembly together on the downswing. Any improper tension or positioning can lead to club-head throwaway and an incorrect downswing plane. The right elbow will not completely straighten until after impact. Also, you do not want to intentionally keep the right elbow in at your side on the downswing. This will happen naturally as well. On the backswing, at about hip height, the right elbow will begin to fold in response to the right wrist's cocking motion, and by the top of the backswing it will have folded 90 degrees. Since the power assembly should stay together on the downswing, a 90-degree angle will be maintained by the right arm. By doing this, you will naturally alter the distance your hands are from your body. When this occurs, it gives the appearance that you are intentionally forcing your right elbow into your side. Thus, by simply letting the power assembly stay together on the downswing, your right arm will tuck into your side naturally (see chapter 14 for the right-elbow drill).

7. *Make the back of the left hand square up to the ball so that the left wrist is pronated at impact.* When viewing the pictures of famous professionals in the classic impact position, one of the most noticeable features is that the left wrist is pronated at impact. The photos capture only a split second of a swinging motion. Attempting to mimic that position requires a forced, contrived motion. Rehearsing this type of motion will lead to a deceleration at impact and usually results in a pushed or shanked shot (see chapter 6).

8. *Lift your left heel for extra distance.* Your left heel should not be intentionally lifted on the backswing. This will not give you more power. The lower body should be a base on which the upper body turns. When you start moving that base around (as in lifting your left heel), you are removing your swing's foundation. The only time the left heel should be lifted is in response to the upper body's motion. There are several touring professionals

who lift their heels, but again, it is done in response to the upper body's turning. Moreover, these professionals have been doing this for a long time. What goes up must come down, and their sense of timing in replacing the heel is excellent. If you are an amateur golfer, resist that tendency to raise your heel. It will not give you any added distance; rather, it will throw off your power factors (see chapter 4).

I'm sure you have all been told to use incorrect sources of power. If anyone tells you that you will hit the ball farther by using these parts of your anatomy these ways, don't listen. Golf is a game of technique, not muscle!

Incorrect Reference Points for Power

It is not uncommon for golfers to use certain parts of their anatomy as reference points for proper positioning. For example, if a golfer is having trouble making a full shoulder turn, she might be told to turn her left shoulder toward her right foot on the backswing. This may work correctly for several swings— even several rounds—of golf, but it eventually will cause the ball to sway on the backswing. The same golfer might also be told to turn her left shoulder under her chin to ensure a completed shoulder turn. Often in this situation the golfer will become so focused on having her shoulder meet her chin that she will fail to make any turn. Instead, she will end up making her shoulders touch her chin by simply lifting the club in the air. The following is a sample list of commonly misused reference points that are supposed to generate more power in the golf swing.

The Backswing

Point the left shoulder at your right foot: When this reference is used, it is not uncommon for the upper body to either move downward (a dip) or to the right (a sway).

Turn your left shoulder under your chin: usually causes the shoulders to dip.

Feel your shoulder touch your chin: often results in the arms lifting the club.

Keep your eyes on the ball to keep your head still: This promotes the dipping of the shoulders and a reverse pivot.

At the top of your backswing feel 60 percent of your weight on your right foot: Practice this a few times and you will find yourself swaying.

Point your right knee toward your left foot at the address: This is often taught to prevent golfers from swaying; in reality, it only promotes more swaying. When done enough times, you will find yourself leaning on your left side at the address, which will lead either to a sway or a reverse pivot.

The Downswing

Tuck your right elbow into your side: The right elbow will naturally maintain its cocked position on the downswing if you have proper positioning. By attempting to tuck it into your side, you will end up pushing the ball toward the right.

Try to square the back of your left hand to the target at impact: The downswing moves so quickly, it is impossible to actually square the back of the left hand without losing acceleration. Of course, when you lose acceleration, anything can happen. In this instance, the shot is either blocked to the right or shanked.

Watch the club head hit the ball: This is usually told to keep golfers from lifting their heads on the downswing. If you are swinging correctly, the speed of the swing will be so fast, you should not be able to see the club head hit the ball. If you do, you are not generating enough club-head speed.

Feel your right shoulder touch your chin: This is dangerous. If your shoulders are moving and your head is still, it will be like hitting a brick wall. Constant use of this technique will jar your neck and spinal column.

Make sure your hands lead the club head at impact: This is a great reference for practicing a shank shot, so unless you are trying to learn to shank the ball, forget this one.

You have just seen how commonly used reference points can inhibit the power swing. In small doses, some of these references can be helpful. For example, in the case of the shoulder turn, trying to point the left shoulder at the right knee might initially work if you have trouble turning your shoulders. However, the trouble will begin when you make this motion a permanent reference. This means that every time you make a backswing, you'll think only of making your shoulder point toward your toe. Eventually, this will lead to an exaggeration. You will forget that the original idea was to get your shoulders to turn, not to point toward your toe! This is what happens with

POWER GOLF FOR WOMEN

most of these quick references. You forget the motion they were designed to reinforce (making a full shoulder turn) and instead execute the motion of reference (pointing your shoulder at your toe).

When using certain reference points, you are usually better off focusing on the larger muscles of the body. For example, to get the proper shoulder turn, you might want to turn the upper part of your back toward the target. Using smaller reference points, such as the head, shoulder, elbow, knee, etc., will not reinforce the general motion, but rather just one segment of this motion.

If It Feels Right, It Is Probably Wrong!

If a golfer read that a greater shoulder turn will create more distance, she would probably respond by immediately heading to the practice range to put the new tip to the test. At the range, she might turn her shoulders farther then ever. The problem is, this twisting and contorting will give her the sensation that she is really going to whack the ball. However, her feelings are misleading; the golf swing doesn't work that way. Twisting and turning will generate more force, but it requires more than force to hit the ball farther. As we discussed in chapter 1, there are four different power factors that determine how far the ball will travel. By twisting and turning on the backswing, you will probably hamper at least one of these essential factors.

Occasionally you will get lucky and hit a ball farther than ever. Golf is a game of consistency, and one great shot and twenty bad ones does not make for a good game. Go to your local driving range on a Friday or Saturday night. You will witness a lot of young men trying to impress their dates by trying to knock the daylights out of the golf ball. While watching this, you will also see some very unusual swings. You will see more slashing and hear grunting and groaning as each tries to hit the 300-yard marker. This is very instinctive for these young men. This is their natural manner of generating power. And what is worse, their twisting, contorting, and groaning their way through each shot feels correct to them. There are four factors that determine distance, and the ability to grunt is not one of them. The best advice I can give to a beginning golfer: If at the top of your backswing it feels as though you are really going to whack the daylights out of the ball, your positioning is probably incorrect.

86

Unfortunately, until your body learns to generate power correctly, if your swing feels right, it's probably wrong!

The Balancing Act

There are swings in which accuracy is compromised for the sake of distance. Many of you have seen swings about which you might say, "Gosh, Mary really throws her hips into the shot, and look how far it goes." Or, "Marsha really winds up on her backswing, and boy, does she hit the ball." Often good players use unconventional methods to hit the ball. However, these methods are usually a trade-off for accuracy. I once knew a golf professional who taught women to move their bodies slightly to the right on the backswing. On the follow-through they would then take their weight and move back to the left. Some of these women may have hit the ball farther on occasion, but they were caught in a balancing act. Instead of using proper mechanics for distance, they were using their bodies in an unconventional method. Yes, they hit the ball far; however, this is not any farther than they would if they employed proper swing mechanics. The trade-off is consistency and accuracy. Their swings would constantly be relying on tempo and timing to hit the ball. Using this method, they will tend to hit more erratic shots (going left and right).

Once you improve your downswing technique, you will hit the ball farther. The only problem is that at first you will lose a little accuracy. However, as your swing improves, you will see greater distance, and your accuracy will return. For those of you who are performing the balancing act, never quite sure where the ball will go, good luck, because when you lose your equilibrium, you're going to fall. Remember, sound mechanics are your best bet in golf. It is usually worth your while to scrap your present swing and build a new one with these fundamentals. That balancing act can get a little tiring on the golf course. After all, this game is supposed to be fun.

"Hurry Up and Slow Down"

Have you ever noticed when you drive past a road construction site that there are always signs that display an authoritative Slow? Then, as you get closer to the site, you encounter a worker holding a sign with the same Slow command. Being careful not to jeopardize the worker's life, you slow down even more. And then, as you are about to pass the worker, he starts rapidly waving you on, telling you to speed up! I always find this to be quite humorous. You go to all the trouble to slow to the required speed, only to be greeted by a worker frantically waving to make the cars move faster! Slow down but hurry up. As the driver, you're in a no-win situation; you're either traveling too fast or slow. That's the way I feel when I hear someone tell a golfer to swing harder but don't swing too quickly on the downswing.

Many women have come to me complaining that their husbands have told them, "You're not swinging hard enough at the ball." Yet when they try to swing harder, their husbands say that their "downswing is too quick." This confusion is caused by the misinterpretation of the terms swinging harder and swinging too fast.

Women use tempo and timing to generate power, creating a very smooth motion. When witnessing this, men get frustrated because their natural tendency is to use a strong hitting motion. When a woman tries to hit at the ball with her hands and forearms (like a man), it looks as though she is swinging the club too fast, and she's told to slow down her swing. The reality of the situation is that she is not swinging too quickly but incorrectly. Rather than using your hands and wrists to hit the ball, you should increase the speed at which your arms swing. Consistent distance in a golf swing comes from technique combined with strength, with the technique being more important than the strength. So the next time you hear someone tell you to swing harder, then five minutes later tell you your swing is too fast, let it go in one ear and out the other. Just stick to the technique on which you and your instructor have been working. As you become more confident in your swing, it will be natural for you to swing with more authority. And instead of hearing "Swing harder," you'll hear "Wow, she really caught that one!"

Seeing Is Not Always Believing

Seeing is not always believing, particularly when viewing the golf swing. For example, whenever a golfer really puts her hips into the shot, take into consideration the size of the hips and the amount of lateral movement that created or lessened the appearance of hip dominance on the downswing. Keep in mind that the body is segmented at the address. This permits the hips to turn 45 degrees and the shoulders 90 degrees on the backswing. If you were to take a picture of my downswing, it would appear that my hips were leading with a tremendous force. The reality of the situation is that they only turned 45 degrees on the backswing. Obviously, the hips are much closer to their original address position than the shoulders. Because of this, the first motion many golfers notice and emphasize is the movement of the hips.

In chapter 3, we saw how important it was to segment the upper and lower body. Because different people have different flexibility and builds, the appearance of the turned, segmented body may look different with the individual golfer. For example, some golfers' upper bodies may appear to be more segmented from their lower bodies. The lower body seems more distended from the upper body. This distension is caused by the body's flexibility. It's almost as if the torso were double-jointed. Because of this distension, the lower body's movement will be very noticeable on the downswing. Again, it is not that the golfer is using more hip movement; it just looks that way. We have already seen that hip rotation is not a spinning motion; rather, it combines a lateral movement with the turning of the hips. When you notice hip movement, try to define the movement that you witness. Is it lateral movement you are witnessing or horizontal turning? Even a minimal movement of the hips will appear dramatic, especially for someone who has larger and thus more noticeable hips.

Quick Fixes for Power

Many golf professionals and other well-meaning golfers often offer students a quick fix to acquiring distance, but a quick fix is a temporary solution to a complex swing problem. Nine times out of ten, anyone who guarantees that you will hit the ball farther after just one lesson is giving you incorrect information.

Quick fixes for distance may be fun at first. However, this newly found distance will be accompanied by terrible inconsistency. Generally, these quick fixes are based on tempo and timing. When your tempo and timing are just right, everything will work fine. But if your tempo for the day is slightly off, watch out, because you're in for trouble! Throwing more variables into a golf swing means that many more parts have to work together. An example of a quick fix would be to tell someone that power is generated from one part of the body, let's say the hips. Instructing someone to "throw your hips into a shot" may at first increase her distance, but this improved distance is coming from the additional momentum her body is putting into the swing. It is crucial to time this momentum perfectly; otherwise, you will be looking at a topped shot or one that goes dead right. Remember, hitting the ball a good distance, with CONSISTENCY, is our goal. There are cases in which a fast turn of the hips is an integral part of a consistent swing. This is only true when the movement from one part of the body (such as the hips) affects one of the four power factors discussed in chapter 1. For example, the hips turning quickly will alter the downswing plane by forcing the hands to drop into position. This would be a valid solution for some swings to generate power consistently. Using one part of the body and using its motion exclusively as a source power are not a valid solution.

It is very difficult to get a student to understand basic swing tenets; for example, that the backswing is for position, not for power. Your natural inclination may be to twist your body like a pretzel because it feels as if this will give you more power, but it is necessary to override these inclinations in order to implement the correct technique. When executed correctly, the golf swing is a fairly effortless motion. If you are huffing and puffing after hitting a small bucket of balls, something is wrong. As for quick fixes, everyone who has ever played the game of golf wishes that they existed, but then who can resist a tidbit of advice offered by a friend or professional that guarantees an additional 20 yards off the tee? I guess it wouldn't be reasonable to expect human nature to change for the game of golf!

Change as a Process

I have found that the key to changing your swing is understanding the basic swing motion. The "how" in a golf swing is not as important as the "why." For example, to tell someone how her hands should be positioned at the top of the backswing won't help as much as making her understand why the hands are positioned as such. The most effective manner in which to change one's swing is to view change as a process, not a momentary cure. Part of this process is the rewiring, or remapping, of our former thoughts concerning the swing. Most swing problems begin with faulty swing thoughts. For example, a common but incorrect swing thought used for years was that the right hand should be positioned as if one were holding a tray at the top of the backswing. Since a golfer cannot see her backswing, she would just think of positioning her right hand as if she were holding a tray. The problem is that this puts the right hand in an incorrect position.

Trying to keep the left arm straighter or kicking the right knee in toward the ball at the address may work well for a few swings or even several rounds of golf, but one minor adjustment is not going to permanently change our swings. We have to treat changing the golf swing as a process. This involves a basic understanding of the swing and the role each part of the body plays in the swing. It will also involve visualizing how a correct golf swing should look. And, of course, it involves work on fundamentals and the utilization of good practice—all of which can be found in this book.

If you view changing your swing as a process and not just trying out a quick fix, an entirely different world of golf will open up to you. First of all, when you take the pressure off yourself to find an immediate solution to a swing problem, you will begin to relax. With your body in a relaxed state, your mind can focus much more clearly, and your muscles will be prepared to react to the situation at hand. Change as a process can be viewed as a discipline. At first, it will be hard to discipline yourself, but once you get the hang of it, you'll regret those wasted hours and buckets of balls used while trying to implement the latest cure for your swing. Often golfers get addicted to the process of change so much so that they lose their focus on dropping scores and are content to revel in the enjoyment of disciplined practice and visualization. It is also at this point that your confidence level will soar. No longer will you be focused on the hole-to-hole ups and downs. Rather, you will view golf in a much broader sense of achievement and realize that you are capable of parring even the most elusive of holes.

10

Different Strokes

We all come in different shapes and sizes, with different levels of strength and athletic ability. Because of this, you will see a wide variety of swings, some attractive and fluid, some quirky and unorthodox. As long as a swing is repetitive and provides consistent distance and accuracy, it is a good swing despite how it may appear. The swing that I concentrated on in this book is one that will give you distance and accuracy in the easiest manner possible. Different swings do exist, however, and address and backswing positions can be correct even while deviating from the norm. Some swings seem to work with irons; others, with woods. Sometimes swing differences are caused by an individual's anatomy. This chapter is dedicated to the different strokes that we witness every day in the game of golf.

Anatomical Differences

Whether female or male, each of us is built differently. These differences directly affect one's golf swing, some for the better, others for the worse. The anatomic differences that I am speaking of are length of body limbs, height, and general bodily proportions. I have heard it said that women are not anatomically designed for golf; this couldn't be further from the truth. The fact is, there are certain physical attributes and proportions that do work better in the golf swing. However, these proportions vary with the individual, not the gender. A woman with large breasts and short arms will have as much difficulty swinging a golf club as a rotund man with the same arm length.

Physical differences can affect your address and body positions at various stages of your swing. Let me give you an example of some of the problems you may face with certain physical characteristics.

Long arms: This can be a blessing if you are a woman with a large bustline. Their length will make it possible for your arms to swing freely on backswings and downswings without being hindered by the breasts. However, there is a problem that can arise from a longer-than-normal arm length, and that has to do with the backswing. Often there is a tendency for the arms to swing away from the body on the backswing. This will result in an outside backswing path, which will make it more difficult for the hands to get on plane on the downswing. This problem is usually proportionate with your shoulder width. The narrower the shoulders, the more likely the arm's length will have an effect. On the bright side, most of the better players have longer-than-average arms, and if proportionate with the rest of the body, long arms are an asset.

Differences in length between the right and left arms: This will usually affect two areas of the swing: the grip and the backswing position.

Longer right arm: In this situation, there will be a tendency for the golfer to grip the club far into the palm of her right hand, which will increase the right arm's tendency to dominate on the backswing. At the top of the backswing, the right elbow will be in a *V* rather than an *L* shape. Since the right arm is longer, the left arm may be forced into a straighter backswing position. On the backswing, a slightly longer right arm will offer resistance, which might create an upright backswing path. However, this also depends on grip: Positioning the shaft of the club slightly toward the palm may counteract this tendency.

Shorter right arm: Your grip will tend to be weaker, with the right hand more on top of the club (turned counterclockwise). At the top of the backswing, the right arm will be more inclined to form an *L*. However, since the right arm does not offer much extension, it is more likely for the left arm to be in a bent position. With a shorter right arm, the club may be swung on a more inside backswing plane. However, the grip, if in a weaker position, might counteract that tendency.

The legs and hips: When one leg is slightly longer than the other, a problem with the weight distribution at the address can occur. Often the length difference is not a function of the actual length of the leg as it is of the hip. In many people, one hip is slightly lower than the other. There can be many reasons for this, including the aging process and mild arthritis. The biggest problem is when the right leg is longer than the left. This difference may only be about a half inch, but it is enough to disturb weight distribution at the address. The right leg, when slightly longer than the left, will cause you to lean onto your left side at the address. When the power center moves to the right, the weight will also shift in the same direction. However, if the right leg is even slightly longer than the left, this shifting becomes difficult. When your power center cannot complete its full rotation to the right, a loss of power will be the result. The solution is to put more flex in your right knee at the address. This correction will put your body in a better position to allow your power center to make its turn. This unevenness can also cause a sway. When weight is on the left side at the address, some golfers attempt to shift the weight to the right by consciously moving it to the right, which of course is a sway. The solution is simple. Add more flex to the right knee at the address to equalize the weight distribution.

The width of the shoulders: The physical symmetry of the body is very important. The width of the shoulders and the size of the hips should be proportionate to body length. Some women have narrow or weak shoulders. With this physical build several problems can arise. First, the hands (picking up the club) or forearms (arms swinging outside their backswing plane) will tend to dominate on the backswing. Second, without the width or strength in the shoulders, it is not uncommon for the golfer to lift herself out of her posture on the backswing because the shoulders cannot supply an anchoring effect. For exercises to increase shoulder size and strength, see chapter 14.

A Woman's Anatomy and the Golf Swing

Many women have been told, and believe, that they are not anatomically designed for the golf swing, but in reality, women have a greater natural aptitude for the golf swing than men because of a woman's physique. When performing an athletic feat, it is natural to want to use the strongest part of one's body. Because women lack the forearm and hand strength of men, there is a subconscious effort to use tempo, timing, and technique to hit the ball. These are the same factors that are necessary to execute a good golf swing. Most men try to generate power with their hands and forearms in a slashing motion. It is true that with such brute force the ball will travel a decent distance, but rarely with any degree of accuracy or consistency. Their strength will make it harder for these men to override their natural instincts and thus more difficult to learn the techniques of a good golf swing.

In chapter 3 we discussed the stabilizing feature of the power anchors. For women, the hips are a natural power anchor. A woman's hips are usually wider than a man's. This width creates a lower center of gravity, which permits greater stability throughout the swing. The only reason the hips have hampered a woman's golf swing at all is that women have traditionally been taught to use their hips incorrectly.

A woman's breasts can interfere with the golf swing, but only on rare occasions. I think that much of the interference by the breasts is psychological, particularly for the beginning female golfer. Many beginning female golfers feel uncomfortable when first gripping a golf club because they are not sure how to position themselves in relation to their breasts. Male golf professionals often are uncomfortable addressing this subject, so the woman is left to figure it out on her own. "What do I do with them?" is not an uncommon question from a beginning female golfer. The answer to this question will depend largely on arm length and bust size. However, and more importantly, at the address, a woman should not view her breasts as a deterrent to a proper swing; rather, as a part of the anatomy that will not hinder the golf swing. At first, the address position may be uncomfortable, but eventually you will get comfortable and not even notice your breasts when you take your stance. You might want to liken this process to when you first grip a golf club. Initially, it may feel unnatural, but after many swings you would not think of holding it any other way.

The hips and breasts have traditionally been targeted as the parts of a woman's anatomy that hinder her ability to perform the golf swing. But as we have seen, the former is an asset, and the latter is rarely a physical problem. As for strength, the lack of forearm and hand strength actually promotes the use of technique. Therefore, if someone should tell you that women are not anatomically designed for the golf swing, let it go in one ear and out the other. If they knew anything about the golf swing, they would realize that it just ain't so.

Weight Loss and Gain

Losing or gaining weight will have an impact on your golf swing. Whenever I hear of a swing that had worked well in previous years but has slowly gone to pot, I observe the golfer's physical stature. Does she appear overweight? Or perhaps unusually thin? Golfers do not realize that a slow gain of twenty pounds or more can completely change their swing. A woman once came to me complaining of a deteriorating swing that had started a year prior to our lesson. It was apparent from her physique that her arms were being hindered from completing the backswing by a rather buxom chest. She told me that previously she had no problem getting the ball airborne and that now it was a difficult task. The only reason that I could imagine was that she had gained some weight. So I politely asked her if she had any major weight change in the past year. She looked at me and said, "In fact, yes. I did put on twenty pounds this year." What had been the cause of her problem was that she had short arms. When she was slender, her breasts were smaller. However, when she gained weight, her breasts became quite large and made it difficult for her arms to swing freely on the backswing.

I have also had men come to me with this complaint. Men have a similar problem when they gain weight. When a man has a shorter-than-average arm length and gains twenty pounds, the weight often takes the form of a potbelly. He is at as much of a disadvantage as our friend who gained the weight in her breasts. Because of the increase in the man's size, he is unable to allow the arms to swing the club freely on the backswing. So it's important to realize that anytime your physique is altered, even from something as simple as a weight gain, your golf swing will be affected.

The Hips as a Power Source

I have tried to emphasize that the hips should not be regarded as a direct source of power; rather, as an anchor creating torque, an indirect source of power. Now I am going to throw you for a loop.

The swing this book offers is one that will provide the most consistent results for the majority of golfers. However, everyone is different, and it is not uncommon for unorthodox methods to be very effective.

We have seen that the club can take different swing paths back to the ball and that it is not uncommon for plane shifting to occur during a swing. The only time the hips can be used effectively as a power source is when they have a direct effect on determining the downswing plane on which the club will travel. When the hips initiate the downswing, a common reaction is for the arms and hands to drop onto a flatter swing plane. When this occurs and the club is placed on its most powerful path, the swing will create a very powerful shot. In this instance, the hips were used to enable a power factor. The only problem with this is that anytime you rely on the hips to create power, you are relying too much on timing. In other words, if the hips move too quickly, the club face will be left open at impact. If the hips do not move fast enough, they may put the arms and hands on the correct downswing path. Taking all this information to heart, the hips act much better as an anchor than an initiator of the downswing.

The Legs as a Power Source

As with the hips, the only time the legs function as a direct source of power is if they directly enhance one of the other power factors. A strong leg drive on the downswing can be very effective for achieving distance. However, to do this, the legs must facilitate your other power factors. As in with the hips, if the leg drive alters your swing plane, which in effect increases your club-head lag pressure, it will be a benefit. Conversely, if too much leg drive is applied to your swing, a loss of distance will result. As with the hips, a strong leg drive is dependent on timing. Your timing, when off, could result in trouble.

"Why Can I Hit My Irons but Not My Woods?"

This is a frequently asked question. It's easy to blame the club, but unfortunately it's usually not the club's fault. Most likely it's your swing's mechanics.

It's not that your swing changes (although sometimes it can) when you switch from a wood to an iron. The difference between your irons and woods is in the club's downswing path. If you are having a problem hitting your woods but play your irons well, your club is probably taking a severe outside-to-inside downswing path. Let me explain why this works for the irons and not for the woods.

An outside-to-inside downswing plane applies a descending blow to the golf ball. When hitting a wood, we position the ball in a straight line with our left heel in order to catch the ball on the upswing (see chapter 3). With our irons we play the ball more toward the center of our stance (however, still left of the center). The longer irons will be positioned farther left of the center. This is because the iron should deliver a flush or slightly descending blow to the ball. When an iron hits the ball with such a blow, it will impart enough of a backspin to make the ball stay where it lands and enough of a forward momentum to gain distance. Thus, you can imagine how someone with a strong outside-to-inside swing path might hit nice irons. Try this swing with a wood and the results can be disastrous. With a wood, we want to catch the ball flush or on the upswing. If we apply the same outside-to-inside swing as with an iron, we will pop the ball into the air or hit a pulled or sliced shot. All will result in a loss of distance. Now you can see why such a swing works with the irons but not with the woods.

It's the Club's Fault!

Okay, so sometimes it really is the club's fault. The problems we have with different clubs are often psychological. For example, many golfers fear using their driver. Generally, when a golfer takes out a driver, a new set of expectations is subconsciously created. Whether we realize it or not, we put undo pressure on ourselves to hit the ball farther. When this happens, we start using the wrong muscles in an attempt to generate power. Consequently, we do not swing the woods in the same manner as the irons. However, there are physically based reasons for our fears.

First, the driver is the longest club in your bag and has the least degree of loft. The more loft, the more forgiving the club. Consequently, the driver will be less forgiving. Also, because of the length of the club's shaft, it should generate the most club-head speed. As we saw in the section on ball spin, the greater

POWER TIP

Another distinction between the woods and irons is that you are more severely punished for an improper swing plane by the woods than with the irons. The shorter clubs have more loft and as such are more forgiving. They also generate less club-head speed. This means that if you hit a seven-iron with the same swing that produced a slice with a driver, the ball will not slice but will probably fade.

the club-head speed, the more spin imparted to the ball, and the greater the chance for the ball to miss the fairway. Moreover, anytime we have an object extended farther from our body, there appears to be a lag time between the body's movement and the object. For example, if you place a very short club in your hands and swing it back and through, the speed of the swinging club will be close to your hand speed, and you will have more control. As the club gets longer, the club head has a greater distance to travel than the hands, so control lessens, and the element of timing becomes more crucial.

There is also a very subtle distinction between the muscles used to hit the irons versus those used to hit woods. The woods tend to be hit with the larger muscles, while the irons use the smaller ones. Again, this distinction is very discreet, but it does exist. For proper execution, the shorter irons, particularly the seven-iron through pitching wedge, require the finesse that the smaller muscles provide. Since more momentum and power are required for the wood shot, the larger muscles tend to dominate. Thus, there is a slight difference when swinging a wood as opposed to an iron.

Another common problem is the club itself. Quality control by club manufacturers is not always the best. Clubs come in different shaft flexes. For example, a woman's club is supposed to be more flexible than a man's, the reason being that the average woman does not generate the same amount of club-head speed as the average male. Supposedly, the flexibility in the shaft will supply additional kick, which will give greater club-head speed. However, women's clubs are often really low-end men's clubs with more stiffness in the shaft than the average man would use.

Manufacturers often gauge a shaft's stiffness by its weight. This is the easiest method of sorting shafts. The more the shaft weighs, the stiffer the shaft's flex. However, weight alone is not a determinant in shaft flex. True flexibility can only be established through correct frequency matching. This tests the vibrations per second of the club's shaft and matches it between clubs. In other words, it is quite possible that a woman may be trying to hit an iron which is actually stiffer than most men's clubs. Because of the stiffness in the club's shaft, the shaft will add little kick on the downswing. Thus, it may be difficult for the club head to square to the ball, and the result would be a shot hit to the right. Conversely, a man may be using a woman's shafted club that has too much kick. In this case, the ball may hook.

POWER TIP

If you hit long wood shots but have a difficult time making decent contact with your irons— particularly the shorter clubs—you are probably using too much body movement in your swing.

So as much as you hear that the game of golf is "all between the ears" or "all in your head," it is quite possible for it to be "all in the clubs." However, the only way to know is to learn about and improve your golf swing. I would recommend seeking a professional's advice. A good golf professional can swing a club and immediately have an idea of its weight, shaft flex, and overall balance.

Why Do I Hit All My Irons the Same Distance?

Another frequently asked question by female golfers: "Why do all my irons seem to go the same distance?" It is not uncommon for many women to see very little difference in yardage between irons, with the maximum distance usually coming from their five-iron. It is also not uncommon for men and women to see very little difference in distance between woods. In fact, the five-wood and the driver may seem almost equidistant.

Club-head speed is the speed at which the club head is traveling at the moment of impact. This impact speed gives the ball its momentum and subsequent distance. Each club is designed to hit the ball a specific distance, and that distance is dependent on the individual golf swing. Most men hit the ball in 8-yard increments. For example, if they hit a five-iron 150 yards, they will use their five-iron if a shot requires 150–158 yards. However, if the shot requires 159 yards, they'll reach for their four-iron. The average woman hits her five-iron 130 yards with 4-yard increments. So if a woman is 130–134 yards away from her target, she will reach for her five-iron. If she is 135 yards from the green, she will use a four-iron. Bear in mind that these are averages. Men and women vary, so the average may not apply to you. The reason for this difference is club-head speed. The greater the club-head speed, the more difference you will see between, let's say, a five- and six-iron. Because men are stronger in the forearms, they can generate club-head speed without much technique. Therefore, you see a difference in the length of the shot between irons (but not necessarily between woods). Since women do not have this forearm strength, they must rely on technique. Many women have been so poorly instructed about what creates power in the golf swing that often their technique detracts rather than enhances their club-head speed. Consequently, you will see little difference in distance between irons and even less between woods. Experiment for yourself. Take a seven-iron and apply a very slow, smooth downswing, intentionally trying not to generate club-head speed. Notice how far the ball travels. Now take a five-iron and apply this same swing. You should see very little change in the distance.

With each golfer's swing, there is a club which will reach maximum swing speed. Ideally, this club is the driver. However, in the case of slow club-head speed, it will be the five- or three-wood. Slow club-head speed usually means that a great deal of casting has taken place. This casting will affect other power factors, such as the area on the club's surface that strikes the ball. In other words, chances are the ball is not being hit in the sweet spot. It will also affect the club's downswing path, usually forcing the club on a severe outside-to-inside path back toward the ball. Also with this type of swing, the increase in the length of the club's shaft with the different clubs will have very little effect on increasing distance because there is not enough energy being created for the shaft to provide additional club-head speed.

The five-iron often provides the correct shaft length, and the club head has enough loft that it will also provide a greater sweet spot. So among the irons, the five-iron usually supplies the maximum distance. With the woods it is usually the five-wood that gives the most distance. The reason is the same as with the five-iron; it is the correct shaft length in combination with just the right amount of forgiveness in the club's loft that makes this the club of choice. It is not uncommon for many men to see little difference in distance between either their three-iron and driver, or three-wood and driver. The brute force that they are applying to a long iron or a high-numbered wood will provide the correct amount of shaft length and forgiveness in the club head that enables them to get maximum distance.

Instead of investing in the latest club technology, your golf game will be far better served if you invest in a series of lessons from a qualified professional. When you start to employ the proper swing technique, you will slowly generate more club-head speed, and you will see greater yardage differences between the different clubs. If you should ever hear a professional tell you that as a woman a 4-yard difference is the maximum distance you can expect from your irons, immediately seek a new professional. Distance has to do with your club and your swing's technique, not your gender. After all, your clubs don't know whether you're male or female.

11

The "Long and Short" of It

I'm sure many of you have been told, "Don't worry about your long game; it's your short game that counts." Nine times out of ten you have been told this because the golf professional believes that a woman cannot hit the ball any measurable distance. This book has proved that is not the case. However, the fact is that male or female, the short game is extremely important. Usually, with women the short game is overemphasized, while men suffer from its lack of emphasis.

So far, this book has offered instruction on how to increase your distance. However, power golf in terms of distance is only half the game. To play a powerful round of golf, you must have a powerful short game. This means having a confident, assured stroke around the green. A purely hit wedge shot has the same efficiency as a powerful, purely hit tee shot. The ball may not travel the same distance, but keep in mind that the wedge is designed to travel a short distance, and by hitting it well, you have gotten the most power and efficiency out of your swing.

The Great Equalizer

The short game can be the great equalizer for those golfers, men and women, who do not hit the ball any measurable distance. However, it is important to have the proper mind-set when working on your short game. To think of the short game as the only place where you have a chance to do well is wrong. The short game is extremely important, but do not try to have your entire game revolve around the green. You must have the distance off the tee and in the fairway to get to the green. Professional golfers usually dedicate 70 percent of their practice time to the short game. Yet these pros are somewhat assured that most, if not all, holes can be reached in regulation. Golf loses its enjoyment when you hit the ball in increments of 125 yards with your woods! So for most women I would emphasize that 60 percent of practice be spent on swing technique (the power swing) and 40 percent on the short game.

It is wrong to believe that women have a better short game than men. In fact, it is often worse. You have to realize that half a wedge shot is just a part of the full swing. If your full swing is incorrect, chances are your wedge shot will also be incorrect. In other words, the same faults that are keeping you from obtaining distance in your full swing are probably the ones that are causing problems in your short game. For this reason I will address the short game and try to illustrate how the power swing and the short game are intertwined. It is hoped that after reading the rest of this chapter you will realize that the long and short of it is— it's all important!

The Chip Shot

The previous chapters have been dedicated to the full swing. Now we will discuss the shortest swing, the "chip shot." The chip shot is used from the froghair (the short grass that separates the green from the fairway and rough) up to 5 yards off the green. The idea of the chip shot is to provide just enough of a loft to carry any obstacles that may lie between you and the green, which is usually grass. A chip shot is commonly executed with an iron. You choose which iron to use based on how much loft will be required by the shot. For example, a "bump and run" is a shot that requires very little loft and a lot of roll. Due to the small amount of loft on the club face, a longer iron would be the club most appropriately suited to the task.

On a chip shot, the same basic stroke is applied no matter which club is used (unless, of course, it is a specialty shot). The chipping stroke emulates the same full-swing motion of the arms and hands through impact. In other words, during a chip shot we are applying one portion of our full swing. That portion is approximately a 2-foot backswing and follow-through. On this

POWER TIP

Most golfers open their stance for pitched and chipped shots. For the chipped shot, an open stance enables you to get a better view of your target and ensures that the hips will not interfere with the swinging arms.

POWER TIP

When performing a chip shot, the most commonly misused swing thought is that of a pendulum. Your arms and shoulders acting as a pendulum replaces your "feel" or "touch" for the shot with tension. If you are buxom, this swing thought will be devastating because your chest will become involved with the chip shot. When this occurs, the arms cannot swing freely.

POWER TIP

When executing the chip shot, most golfers stop or slow down through impact. This feels as if it gives you control through the shot, but unfortunately this is not the case. Be sure you always follow through.

shot, the hands will move with the club head in the same manner as in the full swing.

When addressing a chip shot, your feet should be positioned a little less than shoulder length apart. This position sends a message to the subconscious that you are about to create a very small motion. Your feet wide apart sends a message that you are planning to make a big move. You need your stance to provide you with balance. Because of the delicacy and touch involved in this shot, you would benefit by narrowing your stance. If your feet are closer together, the ball will be approximately in the center of your stance. Your grip and stance will be the same as with the full swing.

Since this will involve such a tiny swing, you might want to choke down on the club (grip more toward the metal shaft). Regarding your stance, it will be very important that your body is segmented correctly, as in the full swing (see chapter 3). Proper segmentation will occur by bending from your hips and flexing slightly at your knees. When this is done, your upper body can move independently of the lower body, which is vital for a well-executed chip shot.

The distance your chip shot travels should be controlled by your backswing. If you want to hit the ball a short distance, use a short backswing. To hit it farther, simply increase your backswing. Going hand in hand with the backswing is the follow-through. You should allow the club to follow through the same amount as it was swung back. The essential part of the chip shot, as with the full swing, is acceleration. If you do not allow the club's follow-through to be more than, or equidistant to, the backswing, the club will decelerate, which will cause a mis-hit shot.

The length of the backswing will determine how much of a shoulder turn will be involved, since on a chip shot, the club's backswing is only a couple feet. Obviously, power is not our goal, so the shoulders/power center will have very little rotation. However, it is important for a little rotation because the shoulders act as a guide for the club's backswing path (see chapter 4). On a chip shot you should never have to worry about the shoulders turning when the arms swing to the right. It should happen naturally. Again, the shoulder turn is minimal.

Basically, we want the arms, hands, and club to swing to the right and then back through toward the left. The club moves in the same manner as it did for the first few feet of the full backswing. The most important part of this motion is that the hands move with the club head. As in the full swing, it is not uncommon to see golfers use their wrists in an attempt to hit the ball. Since the wrists do not cock on this shot, it should be easier to keep the wrist element out of the stroke. The lower body should be still and well anchored. Only on the follow-through of the chip should you feel a little movement, and that will be toward the left. The farther the backswing, the more the club face will open so that the toe of the club will point toward the sky. On the follow-through, as in the full swing, the club should not point directly toward the target past the point of impact (unless, of course, it is a very short stroke). But again, depending on the length of the backswing, the club's toe will again point toward the sky.

Most mis-hit chip shots are the result of taking too much or little of a backswing. The trick in the short game is knowing how much of a backswing to take. This can only be accomplished through practice. Once you have the correct chipping stroke, practice the amount of backswing necessary for different distances. Also, try using different irons and see the effect that the loft of the club has on the ball's distance and roll. The chip shot is usually a small stroke, but an additional inch on the backswing can equal an additional yard's worth of roll, which could mean a missed putt. As you move farther from the green, you will need more of a backswing and less ball roll. This is where the pitched shot comes into play.

The Pitched Shot

A pitched shot should be a lofted shot. The pitching wedge is specifically designed for this shot. Next to the sand wedge, the pitching wedge has the greatest degree of loft and the shortest shaft length of the irons. As such, it is designed to go the shortest distance, with the highest trajectory. There are two reasons why you would want to pitch the ball. The first is if you have an obstacle, anything from a tree to a mound or a sand trap, that you must avoid. The second is that you want control over the ball when it lands. When a ball travels high into the air and then drops straight down to land, it will not have much forward momentum, and as such, it will "sit" upon landing. This is precisely the control necessary for accuracy around the greens. You have to consider that if a green is 40 feet in diameter and the flag is placed in the center, this gives you only 20 feet in which to land the ball without traveling past the flag stick. If you hit a

POWER TIP

If, during a chipped shot, you keep the butt of the club pointing in the vicinity of the center of your stomach, your shoulders will have made an appropriate turn.

POWER TIP

If you tend to use your wrists on the chip shot, you might want to try adjusting your grip. Grip the club in the palms of your hands. This will prohibit your wrist's movement. This grip change should be applied only for very short chips. Do not use this grip for longer chips or pitched shots.

POWER TIP

Open your stance on a pitched shot. In doing so, you will create a steeper backswing and downswing plane. This will put a greater backspin on the ball, which means less roll and more control.

club with little loft, chances are the ball will land on the green and then roll off the back side. However, with a pitching wedge, you have much better control, for when the ball lands, it will have very little roll. Since the ball may roll only a few feet, you can hit the ball below or above the flag stick with assured control. Golfers who have mastered the wedge shot have a truly powerful game. Not only will this ability help them to save par when they are in trouble; it will also put them in constant birdie territory on the par 5s.

The same principles for the chip shot and the full swing will hold true with the pitched shot. The average pitched shot involves anywhere from a quarter to a three-quarter swing. Again, these are just parts of the full swing which will not differ in swing path or execution. Also, as in the chip, distance will be determined by the length of the backswing. And the length of the follow-through should be equal to, or greater than, that of the backswing. If you understand and can execute the full swing, the technical aspects of the pitch shot should not be different. The difficult part of the pitch, as with the chip, is knowing how much of a backswing to take.

POWER TIP

The most common error among golfers is to take too much of a backswing on pitched and chipped shots. Because of this, the subconscious will force the arms to decelerate on the follow-through. This deceleration is responsible for most mis-hit shots around the green.

To learn the correct amount of backswing for pitched shots, practice different-length swings. For example, hit a shot with a quarter backswing; then hit one with a half, and so on, all the way to the full swing. By doing this, you are feeding your subconscious the data it will need for executing a pitched shot on the golf course. Also when on the course, if your pitch shot is too long or short, try to discern whether this was a mental error or an error in technique. For example, the ball lands exactly where it was targeted but due to an exceptionally fast green it rolls past the pin. This is an error in judgment, not with your stroke. However, if you hit a shot which lands past your target, you probably took too much of a backswing.

The short game should be a creative and fun part of the game. Any athletic motion that relies primarily on "feel" or "touch" for its execution also depends on creativity, and the fun part is discovering your creative potential around the green.

An efficient swing is a powerful swing. Energy used in the most efficient manner creates power even if the swing is a simple chip shot with a backswing of about 2 feet. When the ball is struck on the club's sweet spot, even though the result may be a 2-foot carry, it is a product of an effective motion and in that sense is a powerful swing.

Stay Connected

As with the full swing, it will be important to stay connected on the pitch shot (see chapter 6). By this I mean that the hands will move with the club head. Let's use a half swing as an example. When the club swings to about hip level, the wrists should have cocked at least 45 degrees, which equals the amount of wrist cock at the address in the precocked position At this point, the shoulders will have turned about 45 degrees. As in the full swing, on the downswing, when the back of the left hand and palm of the right begin to point down the target line, the wrists will uncock. So at impact the power center will be slightly ahead of the hands and the hands slightly ahead of the club face. As your center continues to turn, the back of your left hand and palm of your right will begin to point left of the target line. Your hands will be in alignment with the club head and the power center until the wrists finally hinge again. Only at the swing's finish, when the wrists hinge, should the club head pass the hands. If the club head gets in front of the hands, you have swung the club with your wrists (see Fig. 44). On the full swing, this leads to a loss of power and accuracy. With a pitched shot, it means less control over the ball's distance and a loss of accuracy.

Obviously power is not our primary concern on the pitch

FIGURE 44. The club head preceded the hands at impact.

POWER TIP

Practice the Y drill in chapter 14. It most correctly emulates the pitch shot.

shot, but accuracy is. With the drive, when you lose power, it does not necessarily translate into a loss of accuracy. For example, if you lose 10 yards on your tee shot, the ball may still be in the fairway (except in the situation where you are trying to carry a water hazard). On a pitched or approach shot, our highly specified target is the cup, so if you lose power, it usually translates into a loss of accuracy. Most hazards are positioned around the green, so a pitched swing that loses 5 yards may just land in the bunker. Or a shot that suddenly goes 5 yards farther may wind up in a hazard on the other side of the green. So you can see that distance equals accuracy for approach, and especially for pitched shots, where there is a very little margin for error. To excel around the green, each shot should be hit with the same consistent swing. If not, it is easy to tally up strokes quickly. It is very demoralizing to use 2 strokes to travel 300 yards and 4 strokes when only 50 yards from the green.

The Sand Game

The Explosion Shot

The shot most frequently used in the sand is the "explosion shot." When speaking of the power game, what better shot to discuss than one with the name "explosion." Obviously the word *explosion* connotes a powerful release, and it is exactly this force that lifts the ball out of the sand. This explosion is not applied directly to the ball, but rather to the sand first and then the ball. The club face will enter the sand first before making contact with the ball.

In discussing the explosion shot, it is important to understand the construction of the sand wedge. As the name implies, the sand wedge is designed specifically for sand shots, but it can also be used off the grass. The difference between the sand wedge and pitching wedge is the club's flange (the flat surface on the bottom of the golf club). The flange on an iron is usually more narrow and rounded than on the sand wedge. On an iron shot, the area responsible for hitting the ball is the club face's bottom edge. However, with the sand wedge, it is the bottom edge and the flange of the club that will cut through the sand. Perform an experiment. Take your sand wedge and open the club face so that the back of the club face points toward the sand. Now let the club touch the sand. Notice the sharp indentation in the sand that your club's flange creates. Ideally, when you contact the sand, it is not only the club face's edge but also the flange that will cut through the sand.

When hitting an iron off the grass, the bottom of the club's face will cut under the ball and through the ground, creating a divot. For sand, which is usually quite soft, the flange of the golf club keeps this edge from penetrating too deeply into the sand. By doing so, the club face is permitted to hit the sand under the ball. Instead of cutting downward, it will enable the club to glide on a more level plane. Sand wedges come in many different lofts and with different-sized and contoured flanges. Some flanges work well in soft sand; others, in hard. Generally speaking, the harder the sand's texture and the more it resembles the ground, the more narrow a flange is required (resembling an iron's flange). For soft sand, the sand wedge's flange will be wider and sometimes rounded.

So now our objective is clear. We want the club's flange to cut through the sand and slice under the ball to provide the ball its lift.

Addressing the Sand Shot

When addressing a sand shot, bend 45 degrees from the hips and grip the club in the same manner as the full swing. If you prefer, you can also choke down on the club's shaft. Because we want our club face in a different position than our regular swing, our alignment will be different. Since the flange is going to cut through the sand, it is imperative that the club face is positioned so that the flange is pointing toward the sand. To put the flange in this position, open the club face about 45 degrees. This means that the club face will now point to the right of your target. To have the club face point toward your target, turn your body 45 degrees toward the left (see Fig. 45). Now your body is in an open position so that the club face will be square to the target line. Your feet should create a forty-five-degree angle with the target line. The ball should be positioned in the center of your stance, and you should dig your feet securely into the sand.

An important distinction between the pitched shot and the sand shot is that at the

POWER TIP

When choosing a sand wedge, you might want to consider the sand's texture on your home course. If the sand is firm, purchase a sand wedge with less of a flange. For soft sand, look for a club with a wider or a rounded flange. Also take into consideration what the sand wedge will be used for. If you plan to use the sand wedge not only for sand but for more lofted pitch shots, then you should purchase a wedge with a flat bottom and smaller flange. A sand wedge with a rounded bottom will bounce on hard ground.

FIGURE 45. When executing a sand shot, the feet should create a 45-degree angle with the target line.

POWER TIP
*Always keep in mind
that when aligning
your body, the club
face must point in the
direction that you
want the ball to
travel (except in
specialty shots), and
the body should
adjust its position to
accommodate the club
head's alignment.*

address of the sand shot you are not permitted to let your club head touch the sand (ground the club). This rule is to prevent you from improving your lie. For example, without this rule you could push the sand away from your ball and position it as if it were on a tee. So when you address the ball, you will have to keep the club head in the air. Also, since you will be hitting the sand first, you will want to position the club about an inch behind the ball and use this as a general area for the club head to enter the sand.

The Execution

The club should be swung in the same manner as in the pitched shot. Whenever you are in a sand trap, be sure that you do not try to hit at or lift the ball with the club head. As in the pitched and regular swing, the hands should move with the club head. Because of the loft of the club and the angle of descent, which is dictated by our address position, the ball will take a very high trajectory. So be prepared to take more of a backswing than you would with a pitched shot. As with the pitched shot, your follow-through should be equal to or greater than that of the backswing. The primary difference between the sand and the pitched shot is that the club head should enter the sand before hitting the ball; this entry point should be approximately an inch behind the ball. Your divot should not be deep; rather, a shallow slice of sand. Again, the flange of the club head is designed to keep the club head from digging too deeply into the sand. However, not even the club's flange can prevent a casted club head from creating a sharp descending blow. With our pitched shot, as we got closer to our target and a lesser loft was required, we chipped the ball. Because of the short backswing required for its execution, rarely should the wrists cock on a chip shot. However, a short sand shot almost always requires some degree of wrist cock. Since the club must enter the sand first, it will require greater club-head speed and a sharper angle of descent than our chipped shot, and this will be provided by the cocked wrists and the open stance. So, on a very short sand shot, instead of using a short backswing, we will simply open the club face as much as possible and take a half swing. With the club face in this open position, the ball's flight should have more height than length, and upon landing, it should "sit" nicely.

Deceleration is the biggest problem in the execution of the sand shot. Since greens are usually well bunkered and surrounded by hazards, the consequences of a mis-hit sand shot can be substantial. Because of this, it is not uncommon for golfers to decelerate on their downswing. When an action is performed slowly, it gives us a greater sense of control. Golfers, fearing the consequences of a poorly hit sand shot, decelerate in an attempt to control or force the club through impact. When decelerated, the club head will pass the hands at impact; this will result in the ball either being topped or hit "fat" (hitting behind the ball). The punishment for a mis-hit shot in the sand is more severe than when hit on a hard surface.

The sand is not a very forgiving place for several reasons. For the club head to travel through the sand, we must take a greater backswing than on a pitched shot. This means that if the ball is hit first rather than the sand, the ball will be sent soaring. Moreover, if the club head should dig too deeply into the sand, the ball may never leave the sand trap.

Once you learn the sand shot, it could quite possibly become your favorite shot. Better players sometimes prefer hitting a shot that is well situated in a sand trap than one that is lying on the grass. The best manner in which to learn to enjoy the sand game is through practice and through understanding what you are trying to accomplish with the sand wedge. I hope this chapter has provided you with that information, but the rest is up to you. If you dread hitting out of the sand, you are missing a very enjoyable part of the game. Mastering the sand shot just gives you that much more confidence in your overall game and can be both a fun and creative part of the game of golf.

POWER TIP

It is very important to keep your body anchored when executing the sand shot. To do this, dig your feet as deeply as possible into the sand and be sure you are bent from the hips at the address. Any slight body movement in the sand can result in a mis-hit shot.

12

Troubleshooting

In golf, you must play the ball as it lies. The more errant the shot, usually the greater the punishment. Out of the desire for accuracy and power in the game of golf arises the need for a consistent swing. The following pages in this chapter have to do with swing problems that will affect your power factors and your consistency. I am sure all of you have experienced at least one of the following problems.

The reverse pivot: The reverse pivot is caused by the incorrect rotation of the power center. Instead of the shoulders rotating on a 45-degree arc in relation to the spine's tilt, they turn on a steeper angle, which allows much less rotation. Because there is not a full rotation to the right, there will be little weight shift on the backswing and a backward (to the right) weight shift on the downswing. There can be several reasons for this incorrect rotation, but usually the source is either the right knee straightening or the shoulders dipping on the backswing (see Fig. 24).

Hitting behind the ball: Hitting the ball fat is a frequent problem among golfers. This is a result of your power assembly disassembling too early on the downswing. The most common fault is casting the club head, caused by the wrists uncocking prematurely on the downswing. Usually, when you hit behind the ball, the club has taken a steeper-than-normal downswing path (outside to inside). You can tell the severity of this outside-to-inside swing by the deepness of the club's divot. The deeper the divot, the steeper the plane.

The reason this is such a common ailment is that unfortunately about fifteen different factors, of which many may be multiple and acting in combination, can be the problem's source. These multiple factors will make it harder to isolate the problem. However, to cure this ailment, realize that a swing fault is forcing you to prematurely uncock the wrists on the downswing.

Topping the ball: Topping the ball, as the phrase implies, means hitting the top half of the ball. The result will be a very low trajectory, or rolling, shot. Casting is usually the cause of both the topped and fat shots. A factor that may determine whether the ball will be topped or hit fat is the club's downswing path. With a topped shot, the club is frequently traveling on a very shallow or flat downswing plane. When the club descends toward the ball on this flat plane, it will hit slightly above the ball's center, which will result in a topped shot.

If you have a chronic problem of topping the ball, the first place to check for an error is on your downswing plane. You may sense that you are making a roundhouse swing; if so, this is probably the source of the problem. Try to be sure that your wrists cock vertically on the backswing, not horizontally (around your body).

Lifting your head on the follow-through: Our upper bodies are at a 45-degree tilt at the address. This is our posture. During our swing, we try to maintain this posture. When your body lifts out of this posture, you will notice your head moving, mainly because your head is your visual center. Common complaints: "My head keeps popping up on the downswing" or "I keep peeking at the ball." Realize that something in your swing has forced your head to move; it is not that you have consciously lifted the head. Trying to keep your head still will often actually force it to move even more.

The three most common reasons for the head's upward movement on the downswing relate to the power center and the power angle. When the power center does not rotate correctly by turning more vertically than horizontally, the head will be forced to move up on the downswing. This incorrect rotation is usually caused by the shoulders turning on too steep an incline on the backswing (see reverse pivot).

In regard to the power angle, it is the premature release of this angle that will force your body to pull up at impact. When the wrists cast the club, the obvious response is for the body to pull up. This is just your body's way of protecting the wrists from being hurt. If your body did not pull up, chances are that the club head would slam into the ground.

Another cause occurs when the shoulders, rather than the power assembly, initiate the downswing. This turn will force the head to move forward and then up on the downswing.

Whiffing the ball: When you miss the golf ball, it is usually the power assembly's fault (see chapter 6). Chances are that your power assembly was never formed correctly to begin with or that it completely disassembled on the downswing. Whenever the club head leads the hands into impact, the wrists are swinging the club (see Fig. 46). When this occurs, there is a high probability that you will whiff the ball.

To cure this problem, try to keep your power assembly together on the downswing and resist the urge for the wrists to 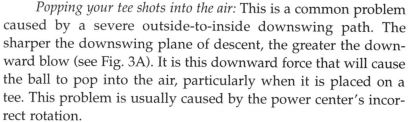 deliver the club head to the ball. The best way to accomplish this is to allow the arms to swing back toward the ball on a plane similar to the club's backswing path.

Popping your tee shots into the air: This is a common problem caused by a severe outside-to-inside downswing path. The sharper the downswing plane of descent, the greater the downward blow (see Fig. 3A). It is this downward force that will cause the ball to pop into the air, particularly when it is placed on a tee. This problem is usually caused by the power center's incorrect rotation.

To cure this, make sure your power center has made its full turn on the backswing. Too vertical a turn by the power center could create a sharp descending downswing blow to the ball. Also, be sure your power assembly is not disassembling too early on the downswing. This could force the club to take a severe outside-to-inside downswing path and deliver the resultant downward blow to the ball.

Left elbow breaking at the top of the backswing: Keep in mind that it is acceptable for the elbow to bow at the top of the backswing; however, we do not want it to break. Usually, when the left elbow breaks, there is a problem with the formation of the power assembly. Be sure when you form your power assembly

FIGURE 46. The wrists are swinging the club head.

that your wrists, not your right elbow, are the first to cock. The hinging by the left wrist should force the right wrist to cock, and then the right elbow will bend. When the right elbow tries to cock, the left arm will be forced to break. Also, be aware of your grip pressure. If you hold the club too tightly, the wrists cannot bend; consequently, the power assembly cannot form correctly.

Dipping on the downswing: This dipping occurs when your head moves downward, on the downswing. Often it is caused by a subconscious desire to get under the ball. You must realize that the ball does not need any extra help from your body to get airborne. However, this problem can also be rooted in the mechanics of the golf swing. Usually, when the head dips, it is because something has pulled it down, and frequently that something is the improper release of the power assembly. Instead of allowing the toe of the club to point to the sky on the follow-through, the hands force the club to continue to point down the target line. When the right hand stays in this position through impact, it will pull your shoulder and then the head downward. Snapping the wrists at the moment of impact will also cause the right shoulder to dip. (By snapping, I mean that the wrists are forcing the club head to point toward the left immediately after impact.)

Another cause is using a scoop release, in which the right wrist bone pronates after impact, pulling the shoulder downward. To stop this, practice the toe-to-toe drill in chapter 14. You want to allow the right hand to move from a position where it points down the target line at impact to where it points to the left of the target line on the follow-through (see Figs. 48 and 49).

Attempting to swing from the inside on the downswing can also cause such a dip. Be aware that if you just let the club return on the same approximate backswing path, you will already be swinging from inside your target line. However, when you consciously attempt to swing on this path, your shoulder will drop.

The shank: A shanked shot occurs when the ball is hit on the club's hosel (where the shaft meets the clubhead; the heel of the club). When struck as such, the ball will travel almost straight to the right. The most common area for the shank to appear is in the short game (60 yards or less to the green). Although shanking with a full swing may be less common, it is still a severe (and dangerous if someone is standing to your right) problem for many golfers. Shanking is a flaw in a swing's mechanics, and it often becomes a psychological obsession. If you have never shanked the ball, try to imagine how disconcerting it would be to fear that every time you hit the ball with an iron it might travel dead right.

Golfers who don't understand the cause of the shank often assign a sort of mysticism to it. Many fear that if they play with someone who shanks the ball they, too, will begin to shank, as if shanking were some sort of communicable disease. Because of this, golfers who suffer from the shanks are often treated like lepers in the golfing community.

The cause of a shank can usually be attributed to the incorrect formation of the power assembly on the backswing or the hands not releasing at impact. This incorrect formation occurs when the wrists do not cock vertically but instead travel more around the body. As a result, the forearms will rotate clockwise, opening the club face. The golf lingo defining this motion is called "fanning the club." As its name implies, instead of remaining square, the club has fanned open to the target line. Unless the arms rotate back into position on the downswing, the hosel will lead coming into the ball. When the hosel hits the ball, it will jettison directly to the right, which of course is a shank. If you are having trouble with shanking, be sure that on your backswing neither your forearms or wrists are rotating clockwise.

Another common cause of the shank is the club's downswing path coupled with the power assembly's incorrect disassembly on the downswing. When the club moves on a severe outside-to-inside downswing path and the club face points slightly right of the target line, this leaves the shaft's hosel exposed and set up for a shanked shot. The club points slightly right of the target line because instead of allowing the club face to follow the power center's turn, the hands failed to release.

Lifting your upper body on the backswing: It is not unusual for many women to spring upward out of their stance on the backswing. This is often a subconscious attempt to generate power by using the body as leverage. The fault of this upward motion can usually be found in the address or the power center's turn.

When addressing the ball, be certain that you have bent 45 degrees from your hips, not your waistline. This bending should enable your lower body to move independently of your upper body. During your backswing, you want to be sure that your left heel remains on the ground. With your upper body bent and your left heel secure, you should be better able to maintain your posture on your backswing.

Make sure that your power center makes its full 90-degree turn on the backswing. Often when lifting the turning stops, forcing the upper body to lift. Remember that the torso should move from the right to the left, never intentionally upward.

Picking up the club on the backswing: Picking up the club means that the wrists have hinged without the shoulders turning. Usually, the club is picked up at the beginning of the swing, when the cocking wrists initiate the backswing. In order to establish the club's backswing path, it is very important that the shoulders initiate the swing. People who have a chronic problem with picking up the club usually have sluggish shoulders or very strong hands, in which case the hands will tend to dominate. To cure this malady, I have two suggestions: (1) Intentionally try to keep the left arm straight on the backswing. When there is tension in the left arm, it makes it difficult for the wrists to cock. (2) Work with your shoulder rotation on the backswing. As long as the shoulders are moving, the wrists can hinge as quickly as possible. When you practice the shoulder turn, focus on the power center turning away from the ball. Sometimes thinking of the power center's turn rather than the shoulders provides an easier swing thought.

Trouble finishing your swing: There are two reasons that usually make it difficult to finish your swing. The first is that when you fall backward (toward your right), you create a reverse pivot. The second occurs when your weight does not shift backward but seems to stop moving toward the left at around the impact area. The latter is a fairly common occurrence. Its cause, an improper hand release, hampers the proper rotation of the power center. We saw in chapter 6 how the power center, the hands, and the club head move in relation to one another. When the hands throw the club head forward at the release (see Fig. 46), the hands will decelerate, and in relation to the hands, the club head accelerates. When this occurs, the connection between the power center, the hands, and the club is lost; consequently, there is no momentum pulling the body toward the left. A great exercise to help correct this problem is the Y exercise (see chapter 14). When you perform this exercise, the hands will move with the club head.

PART II

The Psychology of a Powerful Swing

13

The Powerful Mind

We have all heard the expression "Golf is all between the ears," and in many respects this is true. Perhaps this is why golf is one of the most intriguing and addicting games. The mental side of golf has a direct correlation to the physical, and vice versa. On the physical side, we emphasize good swing fundamentals as a means by which to improve our game. However, we often neglect to emphasize the psychological fundamentals that are so essential to a good golf game. A good psychological perspective is as essential to a good golf game as going to a driving range and hitting golf balls.

In the introduction, we discussed the importance of changing one's mind-set to expect power. In this chapter, we will discuss the basic golf psychology that is essential for improving distance in your game. Many golfers have already mastered certain swing fundamentals but are clueless when it comes to psychological principles. Golf's psychological principles are based on the understanding and reasoning behind the motivating factors that affect your game. Any golfer trying to hit the ball farther without being aware of these principles is only learning half the game. As you read the following sections, I think all of you will relate to, or identify with, the situations discussed.

The Comfort Zone

Have you ever felt as though you always seem to shoot the same score no matter what you do? Let's say you shoot in the low 100s on a regular basis. Have you ever had days when you are hitting your woods well but can not hit an iron to save your life. Have you ever felt that without those solid wood shots your score would have been 120? When your long game is off, does your short game magically pull you through? If so, you are playing in your comfort zone.

When a golfer becomes accustomed to shooting a certain score, there is often a subconscious desire to continue scoring in this range. It is not uncommon for one area of the game to elevate or lower its level of performance to make this possible. Don't get me wrong. There are times when nothing goes well and you feel that you're in the twilight zone! Hitting everything perfectly so that it seems as if nothing can go wrong is referred to as being in the "zone," but most of the time your game will reside in the comfort zone.

Players who feel as though they could shoot 90 or 110 also reside in the comfort zone. Just because they are not shooting a consistent score (by consistent I mean a variance of 8 strokes), they are consistent in the fact that their scores vary to the same degree (around 90 or 110). Golfers who play different tees on a regular basis will notice that somehow they manage to shoot the same approximate score, whether they are playing from the blue, white, or red tees (provided they hit the ball an ample distance to play competitively from these tees). Someone who shoots in the upper 90s and plays from the white tees may expect to see a dramatic decrease in score when they play from the red. Unfortunately, all of a sudden their putting will go, or they will start to hit errant tee shots. Again, this is just a subconscious effort to play within the comfort zone.

As with any unstable lifestyle, erratic golf can be very disconcerting. There is a human need for consistency, and it is out of this need that your comfort zone develops. But how does one go about changing one's comfort zone?

Besides changing your psychological perspective there are some physical adjustments that can facilitate this psychological change. Perhaps the best manner to overcome this syndrome is to play a shorter course. By doing so, you will learn to expect to shoot a lower score. If you play from the white tees, try to play two or three times a week from the reds. Not only will this strengthen your short game; eventually you will begin to shoot lower scoring rounds. As a result, the first time you shoot 89 from the white tees will not be as difficult to accept because you have been shooting in the upper 80s from the red tees. If you play constantly from the red tees and do not have a shorter course to move to, play the whites. You might ask why, since you'll just shoot a higher score, but the odds are against you. However, this is just what we want. You have to shake up your comfort zone. When you shoot from the whites with a higher-than-normal score, you throw your comfort zone out of equilibrium. When you move up to the red tees, not only will it now seem much easier (because you have been used to a much farther length from the whites), but by shaking up your comfort zone, you should now be able to shoot a much better golf round.

So remember, if you are stuck on one of those great plateaus (a low 90s shooter wanting to shoot in the 80s), longing to move to the next level, work on your swing mechanics. But more importantly, push yourself out of your present comfort zone and find residence in one that shoots a lower score. I think you will find the new zone much more comfortable than the old!

Golf Esteem

To move out of your comfort zone, you will also have to change your expectations of your performance. Let's say that you almost always shoot in the 90s. Whether you realize it or not, you probably view yourself as a 90s player. This is where your golf esteem comes into play.

Golf esteem is the golfing version of self-esteem. Golfers with low esteem punish themselves on the golf course. High-esteem golfers do just the opposite: They approach each hole as if it were their first, leaving their bad shots behind them. To raise your golf esteem, you must convince yourself that you are, and deserve to be, an 80s player.

I'm sure everyone has heard someone call herself a name on the golf course. Maybe she has just missed an easy 2-foot putt and you might hear her say, "Oh, that was really bright! Only a moron could miss that putt." Or as the ball goes soaring into the woods on a tee shot, you might hear: "How stupid can you get? Jeezh!" Well, this self-flagellation does not improve your golf esteem. Try to be nice to yourself on the golf course. Start viewing yourself as a better player and don't be shocked when birdies occur; expect them. When you set up for a tee shot, do not think, Oh, please let me par this hole. Think, I'm going for a birdie. And above all, don't keep looking at your scorecard, anticipating what you will shoot. Instead, play each hole as if it were the first. If you're not performing as an 80s player, at least act the part. Eventually, your game will catch up to your mental attitude. If you are taking lessons and practicing, tell yourself that you deserve to shoot in the 80s. Convince yourself that no one deserves it more than you. I'm not asking you to be cocky. . . . I'm asking you to be confident. Chances are that you do deserve a better score. Just the fact that you are reading this book tells me that you are someone who is serious about improving your game.

Permeability

A golfer's permeability refers to how accepting she is of leaving her comfort zone. For example, I once taught a woman who was a good golfer, shooting in the mid-90s or better, on an extremely difficult golf course. One factor that made the course so difficult was its distance from the red tees. Although she played a game that most would be happy with, she was dissatisfied with her length off the tee. One day she said to me, "You know, I score well and have won many events, but I don't want to continue playing unless I can get some distance off the tee." I told her the changes she needed to make would be extensive and could be difficult, leading to many bad rounds before it got better. She told me she had a series of matches coming up. I warned her to wait until after the matches to change, but she said it had to be now or never. Begrudgingly, I started making changes in her swing. She had never made such drastic changes in her swing before, and though I told her it might get terrible, she and I did not realize the extent of the effect it would have on her.

One of the reasons this woman was such a good player was that she was a good competitor. She was just plain gutsy. When the chips were down, she would rally around the flag and pull through with an acceptable score. She had one of the best abilities to stay in her comfort zone that I have ever seen. Off the golf course, she had a very comfortable, regimented lifestyle that did not change much. She had worked at the same job for the past twenty-five years. Her husband and she raised their three children in the same comfortable, predictable lifestyle to which she was so accustomed.

At her club she had obtained a position of reverence among her fellow golfers, who were all amazed at her ability to continually shoot such consistent scores. But several days before her first tournament we made some serious changes. Again I warned her of the possible ramifications, but she stood her ground and said, "I don't care. I just have to hit the ball farther. I can't bear to watch everyone drive the ball fifteen yards beyond me." The tournaments in which she was scheduled to participate took place twice a week for the next three weeks. After her second tournament I received a panicked called from her, begging, "Please help. I'm a disaster. I have never played so poorly!" We met for the next lesson, and I explained to her that this was normal and that playing in a high-pressure situation was making the changes that much more difficult. By her fourth tournament I had never seen anyone so distraught over the game of golf. She was stuck. She could not go back to her old swing, and at the same time she had no feeling for her new swing! This once-gutsy woman had completely fallen apart on the golf course. There was no more rallying around the flag. Every swing that she made was panicked, like a drowning person grasping anything that would float. By the end of the matches she had managed to win as many as she had lost, but her confidence was shattered.

This is a perfect example of a person who is so stuck in her zone that catastrophe resulted when she tried to move to another. She was used to things going along at a comfortable pace and had no idea how to react when the wheels fell off. She was not, as we might say, permeable to change. As a matter of fact, change was a very frightening concept for her. Another golfer might have had the same experiences but not have been as rattled; coming out of the comfort zone might not have been as threatening. So you can see how an individual's psychological acceptance can help or hinder this process. The impermeable woman ended up learning to let go of her comfort zone. At first, her scores got higher, but as we progressed, she slowly acquired the distance she so desperate wanted, and her confidence returned twice as strong as before. The reason she was more confident was that she had experienced the feeling of total futility on the golf course and managed to succeed. Having done this, she now adopted an attitude that she could change anything and do so successfully. I am happy to say that she has dropped 5 strokes from her handicap. She is now a much more permeable golfer. No longer stuck in her comfort zone, she is looking forward to lowering her handicap even further!

A Golfer's Purgatory: Changing Your Swing

The expression "Sometimes things get worse before they get better" must have been uttered by a golfer. Golfers often schedule lessons expecting to see immediate progress. However, this is rarely the case. Depending on the situation, a series of lessons, sometimes months or years of lessons, are necessary before real progress is made. After one lesson the average golfer may see progress, but usually this is just a drop in the bucket when compared to the necessary changes. I dread when a golfer comes to me singing my praises after just one half-hour lesson as much as I dread hearing another professional being blamed for the ruin of a golfer's swing. Neither situation is realistic. First, it is very difficult, even impossible, for a qualified instructor to ruin your swing. I can't tell you how often I have had a student come to me on referral because someone else has destroyed her swing. It is important to realize that an average-to-good golfer really doesn't have anything to be ruined (assuming that you are being instructed by a qualified professional). Someone who shoots in the 90s and can't seem to get into the 80s will most likely have a major swing flaw that is preventing progress. When an instructor tries to correct the flaw, things usually get worse, for several reasons. (1) Now that you know your old swing is incorrect, you have lost your confidence in swinging the club, and every swing becomes a forced motion. (2) Making changes to your swing throws off your sense of timing. Usually average-to-good swings are based mostly on timing, not mechanics, so this loss will leave you without a swing. (3) Mentally you have not yet conceptualized the new swing, and without being able to understand it, there is little chance that you can execute it properly. Additionally, you do not yet have the muscle memory to implement the swing. By this I mean you have not swung the club in the correct manner enough times to allow your subconscious to adapt.

The unfortunate (or fortunate) part of this is that you will find that you cannot go back to your old swing. Often golfers will come to me who have pleaded with other professionals: "Please just give me my old swing back" because "at least with my old swing I could play a decent round." Well, my friend, if you are one of those golfers, you must realize that you can never go back. You are now caught in a golfing purgatory, dreaming of shooting wondrous rounds but caught in the hellish reality of playing pitiful golf. Your old swing has left you, and your new swing is nowhere in sight. Take solace; you are one of many. I do not think that there is a golfer alive who has not suffered the pain of changing her swing, and it is for this reason that you should never take a lesson directly before playing in a tournament. The changes implemented during your lesson have a slim chance of making it to the golf course.

It is common for professional golfers to take a year off from heavy competition just to revamp their swings. If this is done by professionals, you should not expect to be any different. When a golfer makes swing changes, she may often appear to take one step forward and two steps backward. Initially, this is quite disconcerting; however, the pattern will change. Your instructor is changing fundamentals of your swing, and without having any consistent fundamentals, you are relying on timing and luck. Thus, if you are taking golf lessons and your swing at first seems to worsen, be aware that your golf professional is working diligently on changing your fundamentals. What you should be leery of is a golf professional who offers a quick fix for your swing. She is giving you something that simply accommodates your swing for the moment, which in the long run will only worsen your swing.

Since the swing is divided into parts (the address, the backswing, the change of direction, the downswing, and the follow-through), the process of changing your swing will involve work on one aspect at a time. This can often lead to a dual swing. The backswing could be your new self; your downswing, the old you. It is a long process before you can escape the old you completely so that the new you can take over. A faulty swing is usually caused by a series of faults that enable you to get back to the ball. For example, your club may be traveling far outside your desired swing plane on your backswing; on the downswing your hips subconsciously move quickly so that the club drops onto its proper path. Here are two faulty moves that have worked together to create a mediocre shot. When the individual decides that she is tired of hitting mediocre shots, she will seek lessons. Most likely the first change a professional would make in such a swing is to get her student's backswing on the correct path. When the student achieves this, the problem will be that on her downswing her hips are still spinning. Here you have the backswing as the new swing and the downswing as the old one. The hips spinning, with the club in the correct position, will result in inconsistent and unattractive shots. Now you have a golfer caught between a heavenly backswing and a devilish move on the downswing. It will take time before the backswing is grooved in sufficiently so that work can be done on the down-swing. During this time, the golfer may suffer some very discouraging rounds of golf. Your instructor can see the light at the end of the tunnel for you because she has taken many other golfers down this path. However, for you it will seem as if you will never be able to play again. As I have said, take heart. You are not the first or the last to have such feelings of futility. If you have a qualified instructor, you are in good hands. She will see progress where you see none. I have often felt that creating a golf swing is like taking a big lump of clay and sculpting it into a work of art. There are different grades of clay: Some are easily shaped, others take more work, but all can be sculpted.

I equally dread claims that after one half-hour lesson I have performed a miracle on a golfer's swing. I wish it were true, but nine times out of ten it is not. (I'm usually only good for one miracle a year.) When someone rushes back the day after a thirty-minute lesson singing my praises, I know I'm in trouble. There are no miracle workers in golf. When people put you on a pedestal, it is unreasonable. They are just setting you up to fall. I have been told by both men and women that have taken lessons from golf professionals around the world that they feel I am the best pro. I accept this compliment with much pride and humility, but I am not the only one in this relationship. Their progress is very much dependent on how well they listen and practice. Unfortunately, a golf professional cannot lay her hands on someone's shoulders and declare, "You are cured. Go forth and shoot par golf!"

I am reminded of an instance that occurred when I was teaching at a private club. A member's daughter had good potential for her golf swing and had received instruction from several top golf professionals. She was about twelve years old, and her father felt she had the potential to make the record books. Because of his strong belief in his daughter's talent, if he felt she was not progressing quickly enough, he immediately blamed the golf professional and moved on to another. When he was in the process of finding another pro, he had heard about me and begged my head professional to fit his daughter into my busy schedule. As a favor to the head professional, I obliged. The young girl was quite nice and had been playing since she was four. Her athletic ability was considerable but not prodigious, and I got the impression that she played to please her father. During our first lesson she seemed very confused about what she needed to accomplish to improve her swing. The reason, I felt, was that her father had moved from so many different professionals that she was just plain confused. I broke the swing into very simple terms and gave her a few innocent exercises aimed at getting her to swing the club but not think the club through the shot. At the end of the lesson I felt as if we had made progress, but in no way did I feel it was a dramatic improvement.

The next evening, as I was waiting for a lesson, her father came bolting through the doors. His face was flushed and his hair disheveled. As I was later to learn, he had just finished playing golf and had rushed over in the hope of catching me. He looked at me straight in the eyes, his head swaying in a motion of deference. I thought he was going to get on his knees! He said, "I want you to know I think you are the greatest golf professional I have ever encountered. What you did for my daughter in one lesson is phenomenal. She had her best round ever, and she was hitting the ball a ton off the tee." My first reaction upon hearing this was, Oh, dear, I'm in trouble. I explained to him that I helped, but I really was not responsible for the great round. However, he would not allow me any humility. He kept saying, "Oh, no, it was all you," and he repeated several more thank-yous as he made his way toward the door. As I was preparing for my next lesson, I felt horrible, for I knew this man was setting me up for a big fall. Yes, I was responsible for part of her score. However, it was just coincidence or her confidence level, or perhaps her timing was good, but it was not mechanics that produced such a good score. I knew that great game would be short-lived because the girl had some serious flaws in her swing that needed to be corrected.

Sure enough, a week later I received a desperate phone call from her father begging for another lesson immediately. On our next lesson the flaws in her swing were so apparent, I felt it was necessary to do some serious work immediately. I explained to her and her father that this would disrupt her game, so they should not be too upset at having some bad rounds. About two days later the father called again and said his daughter was having a terrible time and could I fit her in. Again I obliged and worked with her on her swing. After this lesson I felt that progress was beginning to be made. If she would take a lesson a week, I would probably see the fruits of my labor in a couple of months. Well, unfortunately, that was not to happen. The next time I saw the father he glared at me and told me his daughter was playing terrible golf. He gave me a nasty look and then walked out the door. The next time I saw them, neither he nor his daughter would speak to me. I had to force a conversation. By the end of the following week I saw her getting a lesson from yet another pro. It looked as if she had worked on some things I had taught her, and I knew the other pro would probably get the credit. Quite frankly, I was relieved to see the two of them go. This poor twelve-year-old child may have had talent, but to have had to grow up bouncing from golf professional to golf professional, searching for the miracle worker . . . Golf is a great sport for kids if used properly. It should teach a child patience and perseverance through difficult times and should also instill the importance of developing a solid relationship with her instructor. Believe me, if I thought for a moment I could not help that child, I would have simply referred her to a different professional. Her father felt that teaching his daughter was a golf professional's privilege (considering what he felt to be the enormity of her talent). Even if this child should become a great player, I feel sorry for her. Because the precious self-discovery that golf has to offer is something she will probably miss with her father at the helm.

Your golf professional is not solely responsible for your accomplishments or your failures. You are a team that must endure the good and bad together. Realize that although it most likely will get worse before it gets better, if you have a qualified instructor, she will steer you through uncharted ground and set a course for true improvement.

Using Another's Prescription

I once taught at a driving range in which the golf professionals' teaching area and the public tees were intertwined. As a result, while I was giving a lesson, it was common for anyone hitting golf balls just several yards away to listen to every word I said. I protested this situation because I felt it was demeaning to golf professionals. Plus it was like just giving your best teaching secrets away. Unfortunately, the owner of the range did not see things my way. To him the bottom line was how many range balls were sold that day, and if that person who was listening bought another bucket of balls, he was satisfied.

Several regular range customers would stand next to me as I gave my lessons, listening and trying to implement into their own swings everything I was telling my students. Of course, this infuriated me. Day in and out, these people would get free lessons. Occasionally, I would glance over my shoulder and watch them practice something that I was currently teaching my pupil.

The more I watched them, the more I noticed their swings worsen. They did not realize it, but focusing on the same problems as my student was comparable to taking someone else's medication. A doctor may have prescribed it for the same symptoms as yours, but the illness may be different. If you take another's medication, it may help, do nothing; or make you sick. In golf, it often hurts your swing.

For example, a golfer who has a tendency to use her hands incorrectly on a backswing might listen to a lesson in which I am teaching a student to forward press with her hands. If our "handsy" player tries to incorporate this type of press, serious problems may occur. Often friends who take lessons from different pros will compare notes on their lessons. The difference is, even if they have the same problem, there could be two entirely different reasons for its occurrence.

Golf professionals have a goal in mind for the students with whom they are working. They may take them through various awkward stages with this goal in mind. For others to try to go through these stages without proper supervision is a waste of time. Chances are they will end up ruining, not helping, their swings.

I once knew a golf professional who took his students through the strangest phases. He would have them work on exercises that made their swings look terrible. But he would always have a goal in mind. He could see the light at the end of the tunnel, but his students did not. If his students stuck with him long enough, the benefits were tremendous for some, but others never did seem to get it. The one whose swing never quite jelled would walk away empty-handed. I watched one woman struggle with him for a year and a half, taking weekly lessons. She struggled and struggled, and finally it clicked. I now watch her hit the golf ball with tremendous power and accuracy. However, if you were to watch her lessons or try to implement the changes she made in her swing, you would have been left empty-handed.

So unless you are a true student of the game and want to know the cause and effect of swing problems, do not listen to someone else's lesson. Try to stay focused on that which you are working on. If you are listening to a good professional teach, she will not be generic; she will customize her methods to each individual swing. If you are ever in the situation where you can eavesdrop on an instructor giving a lesson, your temptation to get a free lesson will probably be strong. However, remember that "you get what you pay for." There are no free lunches in the world of golf instruction.

Power Revealed

Power does not reveal itself in the manner that many might expect. Most golfers assume that an adjustment in their swing will instantly bring them an additional 10 yards. Often people will put a time limit on this improvement. Some might expect to see the fruit of their labor after five lessons; others, after several months. The truth is, power is usually revealed in flashes. All of a sudden, out of the blue, possibly after you've completely given up on the idea of hitting the ball farther, it happens.

When the average golfer tries to hit the ball farther, immediately she will start to use the wrong muscles in her body. As she works on her technique, she will train her body to use the correct ones. The problem is that mentally she is still putting a great deal of pressure on herself to hit the ball farther, so there is a tendency to use the same incorrect muscles. Often it is not until she lets go, or gives up that the distance suddenly occurs. This action means she is no longer trying consciously to hit the ball farther (which sends a subconscious message to her body to use the wrong muscles). Instead, the practice sessions using the correct technique and muscles can now dominate because they no longer are interfered with by the conscious mind. When the golfer hits her second shot, the shock from the first shot will most likely have taken its toll. By this I mean that once she has seen how far her ball has gone, she will expect her next shot to travel a longer-than-normal distance. It is this expectation that will get her into trouble because she will immediately use the wrong muscles to try to force the distance that came so easily on the first shot. This usually results in a topped shot or even hitting several inches behind the ball.

There is an old golf hustler's trick that plays on this psychology. When a hustler is playing with someone, he is building a profile of a player's physical and psychological capabilities.

When the player hits a longer-than-normal tee shot, the hustler will move in by saying, "What a great shot! How far did that ball go? I think that must be a two-hundred-fifty-yard drive." The hustler is not building your ego; he is setting you up to fall. He knows that you, as an average-to-better-than-average player, have just hit a shot that is not in your normal repertoire. By focusing on this shot and inflating your ego, he is ensuring that your next shot (or if you get lucky, your third shot) will be mis-hit. He knows your swing's capabilities, and he also knows that when you try to hit the ball farther, you will employ the wrong muscles and mis-hit the ball. The prime time for a hustler to use this psychology is when you have hit a beautiful drive and your approach shot is long and over water. Believe me, that hustler is getting ready to toss you another ball because he knows it is going into the drink. A hustler would not use this psychology on a professional player. When a professional player is pumped, he will continue to hit the ball farther. This is because the professional's mind and body have been trained to create power correctly. So when a professional thinks about hitting the ball hard, he is not employing the same swing that an amateur would. Encouraging comments about the distance the ball has traveled will just give more confidence to our professional player.

It is important to realize how this power reveals itself so that you do not impede its progress. One of the worst ways it can happen is if you have a foursome of men in front of you, at a distance which would normally be out of your range. You feel that there is no problem in hitting the ball, so you set up, and bam, you hit a career tee shot! As you yell, "Fore," the ball lands about 15 yards before the group and then comes to rest 7 yards behind the men. As you yell an apology, the men give you a "don't-do-that-again stare." It is at this point that you forget about being apologetic and think to yourself, If this is what Jane Horn considers to be the worst way power reveals itself, then I would like to know the best—because I feel great!

The Mystical Side of Golf

How often have you heard a golfer utter the expression "If I could only bottle that swing, I'd make a million!" Wouldn't that be wonderful. A potion which, upon consumption, would ensure a flawless day of sub-par golf. I believe that if any true golfer were to invent such a potion, rather then selling it for countless millions, she would hoard the formula so that she and only she had this ability. Gentlemen's game? Baah! The secret would be too great to share.

The mystical game of golf has us praying to the golf goddess for a straight drive and offering sacrificial virgin golf balls (and for the less pious, range balls) to her hungry waters. In its mystical presence the mere sight of trees puts us in a state of total fear and reverence to Mother Nature. For alas, what golfer upon standing in the tee box has not said to herself, Please not in the woods again. Also, in our reverence of nature, on our accomplished scores we have bestowed names such as birdie, eagle, and the ever-rare albatross, while to our mistakes we have given the lackluster, monotonous names bogey, double bogey, triple bogey, and quadruple bogey to describe the futility of our circumstance. What is really behind the mysticism of golf? Are we correct in our perception of the game as both mysterious and confounding? Or are there very simple reasons why a perfect swing is so elusive? I happen to believe that both are true.

Perhaps the most confounding aspect of golf is the knowledge that the same swing can produce two entirely different results. In other words, one day you have it, the next you don't. In many cases, consider yourself fortunate if it lasts an entire day. It is possible to have it on the front nine, only to see it disappear on the back nine. And for some truly manic golfers, it fluctuates from hole to hole. Have you ever thought to yourself after finishing a terrible back nine, How can someone who just had a great front-nine score finish so badly? Often, the only reason is "My swing just left me."

It is not uncommon for superstition to intercede when there seems to be no explicable reason for an event. For example, I played golf well on the front nine because I was playing a number 2 ball. As soon as I lost that ball and started playing a number 4, my game went downhill. You would be surprised (or maybe not if you are one of the superstitious) at how many golfers will only play a ball with a certain number on it.

Looking back on my pro-shop days, I can still see that look of desperation on the face of a golfer coming hurriedly through the door frantically seeking a sleeve of Titliest 2s. If the pro-shop personnel knew that there were none in the display case but that they lay in an unopened box in the backroom, they would shake their heads in a "gosh I'm sorry" manner, refusing to go to the trouble to help the poor soul. I, on the other hand, being a golfer, know that feeling of desperation and would be foolish enough to drop everything to go into the backroom and look for the magical balls. However, the part that I found puzzling was, if the balls were truly magical, why were golfers always running out? If they were coming back for more, this meant that they were losing them. The superstitious have an uncanny ability to rationalize; for example, "I used all the luck in the ball." "It's a known fact that Titliest makes all its numbered golf balls differently, and the number 2 I just lost must have been defective." The amazing part is that these words are not spoken by ignorant human beings. Many a CEO and self-made millionaire have boyishly uttered such a response.

Let me try to explain why the golf swing can be so elusive. One of the problems with golf is that it looks too easy. When the average person sees someone with a fluid swing hit that little white ball a long distance, his immediate reaction is "Hell, I can do that." Let's face it. To play a decent round of golf, you do not have to be in exactly peak athletic shape. And the amount of physical exertion expended on the golf course (other then having to look for your golf ball) is minimal when riding in a cart. So this leaves the game open to many individuals who quite frankly do not have an iota of athletic ability. Because it does not require an abundance of strength or fitness, the sport quite frankly looks easy and attracts participants who are nonathletes. Therefore, you have a group of participants whose expectations are going to exceed their potential for output. Most golfers do not realize that good golf is consistent golf. Golf professionals do not play 18 holes hitting perfect golf shots. They play 18 holes with a consistent swing. This leads us to what I believe to be the explanation for why one minute you have it and the next it is gone: random reinforcement.

Random reinforcement means we are not always reinforced with a good result after having made a good swing. In fact, we can execute a good swing and get a bad result or swing badly and achieve a good result. This scrambles the reinforcement of our actions, which leaves us without rhyme or reason for our result.

Golf would truly be an easy game to learn if every time the ball went to the right or left we knew the cause. Unfortunately, the ball can go to the right for a multitude of reasons. Because we can't see ourselves swing the club (and even if we could, most of us would probably not know what to look for), we cannot pinpoint the problem. This is why both rank amateurs and touring professionals have someone watching and working with them on their swing.

Beginners often find it hard to grasp the concept that their hitting the ball well and its traveling a good distance could be the product of a bad swing. This creates problems for golfers in general, because hitting a good shot with a bad swing becomes reinforced. Often, since we cannot see ourselves, the only way to weigh the merit of a golf swing is on its result. And since the result was good, we of course assume that the swing was good. And when the average golfer hits a ball into the woods with a swing that actually was quite good, he will immediately think that the swing was horrible. This confusion of reinforcement leaves the average golfer in a topsy-turvy state. The professional golfer, however, has developed a "feel" for the swing. She has practiced fundamentals so many times and hit good shots with good swings, reinforced by her teaching professional's feedback, that most of the time she can feel what is wrong with her swing. Also, many times she has reduced the variables in her swing to a minimum, so it is not as difficult to discover the flaw that made the ball travel to the right.

Another problem is that the result of a shot is not necessarily proportional to the severity of the swing problem. You can put a pretty good swing on the ball and still have it careen into the woods. You might ask, How can the swing be considered good if the ball went into the woods? A good golf swing is a consistent, repetitive motion that creates maximum power and accuracy with the least amount of variables vital to the swing's function. It is possible that one of these variables will be slightly off when executing a swing and thus produce a shot that careens into the woods. However, this does not mean the swing is bad. Actually, using the same swing with a minute adjustment in the flawed variable will produce an excellent shot. The punishment for a minute maladjustment in the swing far outweighs the swing's imperfection. We are often severely punished for fundamentally good swings. On the other hand, we can be unduly rewarded for a fundamentally flawed swing.

Have you ever heard the expression "My timing was just off today. I couldn't do anything right"? You'll remember from chapter 1, that good fundamentals create good timing. For some golfers, being slightly out of position on their backswing or downswing actually puts an additional beat in their swing's tempo, which throws off their sense of timing. Tension is a common foe of timing. It is possible for even the slightest increase in tension to affect your swing. Let's say that you are very tense and about to hit your tee shot. You may not realize it, but the tension that you feel has caused your grip pressure to increase, which in turn has created tension in your forearms. At the address, if the forearm muscles are too tense, it is not uncommon for them to try to take control of the backswing. This can lead to a slight change in the club's swing path, usually putting it on a more outside plane. Since the club is taking a more outside path, it will probably take a longer time to reach the top of the backswing (maybe just a second). However, this change in time—although minute—is enough to throw off the body's timing. Think of a car's engine with all the pistons firing in order. One piston off by just a split second will affect the engine's output. This same principle holds true for your golf swing. Thus, one can see that a word like timing, which intimates something magical or mystical, can be directly affected by the swing's fundamentals.

Coincidence is the next factor that elicits mystical responses in the game of golf; it is also the primary ingredient in superstitious behavior. When golfers are having a bad round they will often search desperately for a thought that will pull their game back together. It is not unusual for a golfer to try to implement a cure or quick fix from an article they may have read or to ask for advice from the other members of their foursome. Let's say that a golfer is having a particularly rough day. She may be topping every other shot. Someone in the foursome happens to notice that on the golfer's downswing her head is moving and advises her to try to keep it still. We all know that when the head moves, nine times out of ten it is a swing fault, and trying to solve the problem by keeping the head still only worsens the situation. However, let's say our ailing golfer now concentrates on keeping her head still and she suddenly hits the greatest drive she's ever hit. Now she immediately thinks that she has found the cure. Upon hitting her next drive, wham! It happens again. She now experiences that mystical moment when it all comes together. Yes, this was the answer all along; it was her head. After playing the last five holes beautifully, she feels great. She then turns to her husband and asks, "What time do you want to play tomorrow?"

The next day, our enthusiastic golfer will hit the links with renewed hope and a sense of limitless possibilities. It is possible that she will have a good round. Maybe even her next several rounds will be good, but after that the wheels will again fall off.

Her game will be worse than ever. That her swing came together is an example of coincidence and the effects of timing on a golf swing. It could be purely coincidental that at the moment she thought of keeping her head still her swing improved. It might have been a minor problem that had caused her to "top the ball." Let's say she had been casting the club at the top of her swing. As she started to tire, her casting motion was stopping because it involved too much energy and strength. This all happened at about the same time that she started thinking of keeping her head still. But that keeping her head still really had nothing to do with the change that occurred in her shots; it was just a coincidence. Her endeavoring to keep her head still will eventually paralyze her swing to the degree that perhaps she will top every shot. And now coincidence cannot occur because the swing is too badly damaged.

Timing also may have played a role in our friend's success. We have discussed the fact that our swing has an internal timing, or rhythm, on which it relies. It is possible that by keeping her head still she may have put her body back into its tempo. Once the subconscious could resume its tempo pattern, it enabled the club to get back to the ball. Remember the expression "If I could only bottle that swing, I'd make a million bucks." Well, this is precisely the type of swing we are talking about. It feels great because the tempo is smooth; however, there are no underlying fundamentals to support this tempo. Whatever tempo supplied is keeping the head still will be short-lived because her swing will change and once again negatively affect rhythm, with no fundamentals to fall back on. And the worst part is, keeping the head still will actually destroy other fundamentals essential to her tempo.

All the points discussed in this chapter are precisely the reason we keep coming back for more. What golfer could experience the effortless feeling of a ball well hit and not want to try to replicate the swing's motion? The enticing simplicity of a shot well hit can't help but further convince us that this is an easy game. It is precisely this shot, which may appear once in a round of golf, that seduces us into the land of the mystical. However, as we have seen, much of what exists in this mystical land is firmly rooted in reality. No, I do not believe it is possible to just will yourself into playing better golf. But such a desire, combined with certain swing fundamentals, can create limitless possibilities in your game. However, try to analyze the mystical events that happen to you in golf and root them in reality. A golf game based on superstition goes only so far. As for mysticism, yes, it does exist. Once a golfer has reached a certain level of technical proficiency, what separates the good from the best is the truly mystical part that lies within our subconscious mind.

The Power of Confidence

We have all heard of the power of positive thinking and how confidence is so very important to success. This concept seems to ring particularly true in the game of golf. But what exactly is confidence in golf?

Often golfers mistake cocky behavior for confident behavior. Anyone can get up to the ball and announce to his foursome, "I am going to hit the ball two-hundred-eighty yards straight into the fairway." However, it is another thing to actually hit it that distance. A truly confident person most likely would not make such an announcement. She would be more concerned with the task at hand than with spectators. Confidence is an inner state in which a golfer feels that there is no reason for her not to attain success. A confident golfer does not fear a situation; rather, she embraces challenge. Golf is one of the most humbling sports. One minute you're on top of the world; the next, you're standing on the lip of a monstrous sand trap. When dealing with such extremes, how can anyone expect to be confident?

Confidence does not come from out of the blue. It is earned. You have to believe in yourself and trust your golf swing. To earn confidence, you must place yourself in your feared situation and overcome the fear. Once you have accomplished this, you will be in a position of strength, not fear. A confident golfer possesses self-knowledge. She knows her limitations and also her strengths. Being confident does not mean trying to hit a six-iron when you should be using a five. It involves an inner strength; you expect success and do not fear failure. Confidence in itself cannot create a good shot, but chances are, if you are confident, it is because you have discovered either through practice or play that you can succeed. A confident person does not focus on failure but can fail quite often. The difference between a confident player and one who is not is that the former sees the broader picture. She is excited by attempting something at which she could possibly fail. She continues to strive and places herself in difficult situations because she feels she can overcome or learn by her failures. A person who lacks confidence simply runs from failure. While playing golf, she prays: Please don't let it go into the water or Please let me make this putt, as if someone else is responsible for her swing. A confident individual visualizes where she wants to hit the ball, not where she fears it will go. Confidence in golf is earned only through long hours on the practice tee and playing in high-pressure situations.

The Physical Effects of Confidence

Confidence is not only mental; it can also affect the golf swing's mechanics. Unconfident individuals are those who possess destructive tension (see chapter 2). When you are playing well, you become confident. As you become more assured, your muscles will subconsciously relax. They will not be paralyzed with tension, but will be alert and able to react to the situation at hand. In other words, being confident puts your body's tension in a constructive mode. Have you ever had a day where every swing felt just so easy? That is because when your body is in a constructive mode, it is not working against itself. Instead, your muscles are working together, efficiently, to create an athletic motion.

When a golfer plays poorly, she will quickly lower her confidence level. When this occurs, destructive tension enters the picture. For example, when a golfer becomes uncertain about a shot, her tension level will immediately increase. This increase usually comes out in the grip or the forearms. When the forearms and wrists become tense or tight, it is difficult for the wrists to make their 90-degree cock on the backswing. Let's say you have been playing all day with a normal tension level but your last three drives have gone into the woods. Subconsciously, your tension level has increased. Your grip pressure and forearm tension increase threefold. You are getting ready to hit your fourth drive, unaware of this increase in tension. Because of the amount of wrist and forearm tension, your wrists cock very late, actually at the top of your backswing. This throws your timing off and prevents a complete backswing. Therefore, your first move on the downswing is a casting motion. The club then takes an outside-to-inside path, which results in a huge slice, and once again you are back in the woods. Your confidence is lost, and you feel you are at the mercy of the inexplicable. The more your tension level changes on the golf course, the more likely you are to be inconsistent in your round.

One can therefore see how a confident state produces constructive tension, whereas a state of fear produces destructive tension. Both types of tension have a direct impact on your swing's mechanics. Instead of worrying about your skyrocketing score, you should be focused on maintaining a proper balanced tension in your grip and forearms. This will give you a better chance to revive your swing than prayer.

How to Become More Confident

To become more confident, you must first accept that you are human. Nervous feelings are human. Accept those feelings; do not run from them or be ashamed of them. Once you've accepted them and focused on your task at hand, I guarantee that your anxieties will slowly disappear. The fear of embarrassment is a powerful one, and I think you'll find that what you think is embarrassing others may not. A poorly hit shot is a part of golf. You should not worry what others think, because I guarantee you, their time will come. The people you fear embarrassing yourself in front of are probably worried about their own game. I don't think any golfer enjoys watching someone else suffer on the course. We have all been there and know the feeling of futility. You should be concerned with why you hit the shot that way and then try to get your thoughts back in order. A bad shot for a golfer who is not confident will send her into a tailspin, but a confident player, however upset, is more concerned with the why of the situation than how she appears to others.

Another way by which to increase your confidence is to expect good shots. After you hit a good drive, think of all the range balls you have hit or lessons you have taken that have brought you to this point. Don't assume the attitude, Boy was that lucky; convince yourself that you deserved the shot. Often we are far too rough on ourselves. Remember, do not expect to hit perfect shots. Be consistent. If the ball was well hit and on target, be sure to compliment yourself even if the swing was less than perfect.

As we discussed earlier in this chapter, the punishment for a bad golf shot is often more severe than the swing that caused the shot. In other words, you can make a pretty darn good swing and have a shot careen to the right. Don't place a great deal of emphasis on the shot. The swing was not terrible, just the result. The first thing you should think about is how you are going to get yourself out of this mess, not, How could I have hit such a terrible shot! Such self-flagellation is unwarranted. Also, try to be realistic about your shots. For example, when you make a pitched shot, the ball landing exactly where it was aimed but running by the hole is not a swing fault; it's a fault in judgment. Learn to separate the two. If you make a putt that you believe will break slightly right and it ends up straight, again that is an error in judgment. Also, beware of the rub of the green (bad luck). When you hit a drive that trickles into the deep rough off a very bad bounce, give yourself a break. Don't start getting mystical about the game and assume that the golfing goddess is out to get you. Step back, take a deep breath, and get focused.

Don't get me wrong. Golf can rattle even the most confident of players. But you have to learn to accept the fact that, as in life, some days are going to be tough. On the flip side, it is those beautiful sunny days when we are in the company of friends, when all our putts sink and the ball seems to find the fairway as if it had a will of its own, that keep us coming back for more. The good days really do outweigh the bad. It is precisely this reason that golf has found a place not only in our minds but also in our hearts.

It's an Easy Game

There exist two schools of thought on the simplicity of the golf swing. One believes that the golf swing is a very complex motion. As such, the simplification of this motion makes the swing that much harder to learn. The other school believes that the obsession with the technical aspects of the swing paralyzes the mind and thus impedes the subconscious ability to perform. Alas, it would all be so simple if we could just be like Iron Byron (the golf machine used by the U.S.G.A. to test clubs and balls); unfortunately, the human body, in combination with the human mind, does not function as a machine. Our swing mechanics must be balanced properly with our psyche.

Golf is an easy game if you consider that anyone with any amount of athletic ability can finish 18 holes. And with golf's handicap system, poorer golfers can compete and actually win against better players. But the true difficulty of the game reveals itself as our handicap approaches par.

I have often explained to my students that the closer you get to shooting par golf, the more difficult the quest. For example, if you shoot 160 for 18 holes, knocking 20 strokes off your game really shouldn't be too difficult. If it is, you probably should not be on the golf course! However, if you shoot in the low 80s, breaking into and becoming an upper-70s shooter is a tough, arduous process. Our 160 shooter probably has major, basic swing flaws to shoot such a high score. These flaws are obvious and easily cured (usually by turning the shoulders or using the wrists correctly). If you teach someone who has never turned her shoulders correctly on the backswing the correct movement, she will achieve a drop in score of at least 10 strokes with just that adjustment.

With one half-hour lesson and a few basic instructions, a regular "4 putter" can improve to 3 or less putts on the green, again saving an additional 10 strokes. So you can see how a 160 shooter can drop to the 140s or lower in a week. However, given our 80s player's situation, the problems in her swing are more subtle. It won't be something as simple as turning the shoulders. It will instead be a certain idiosyncrasy in her swing that will be difficult to work out.

Swing Thoughts

A swing thought is a golfer's use of mental imagery to accomplish a specific goal in her golf swing. For example, let's say that on your backswing your wrists are cocking too slowly. You'll want to conjure up an image or idea that will make your wrists hinge faster. One such image is to think of pointing the toe of the club toward the sky as quickly as possible.

Everyone is always searching for that one thought that is going to better her game. Believe me, if that one magic thought existed, it would have been discovered long ago. Swing thoughts can be very misleading. A thought that works today can ruin your swing tomorrow.

I have always found it amazing how people's perception of the golf swing differs. When two people execute the same motion, one might say, "I felt as though I were pushing with my right hand," while the other observes, "That felt as if my left hand were doing all the work." Both individuals' feelings are valid, but they differ in the manner by which they visually and tactically sense the motion. This is where supplying a student with a proper swing thought becomes tricky. You have to try to view the golf swing in the same manner that it is perceived by your student. Catchall phrases, such as "Feel your left arm pull you through the swing," may not work with someone who does not perceive the swing in the same manner as you. A large part of teaching is searching for that one phrase that helps to make it all come together for the student.

Often, it is not that one phrase that has made it all come together. Instead, the phrase has provided a trigger to stimulate learning (spontaneously). Although it may come to you in a flash, it may have been preceded by a mental reconstruction of your swing. This mental reconstruction begins when you take lessons or read or gain any information on the mechanics of the golf swing.

Most people who come to me for lessons are completely lost because what they picture or visualize as being a correct swing is usually wrong. It is almost impossible to take someone who has an incorrect concept of how to execute a golf swing and expect them to swing correctly. Often, I will ask a student, "What are your thoughts when you begin your downswing." If she replies with a remark such as "Getting under the ball," I know she has the wrong idea as to how to execute a downswing. The many "getting under the ball" swings I have seen in my time begin with a casting motion on the downswing, followed by a scooping motion on the follow-through. The first thing I would say to such a student is "you're not thinking correctly. You have to learn why and how the ball gets its loft."

When I first started teaching, I used to have fun trying to get into my students' heads (see the way they were visualizing the swing) and rewire it (change their concept of the swing), all within thirty minutes. This is not an easy task to achieve. Many of the students never even realized that I completely changed the manner in which they viewed the golf swing. The trick is to make it as painless as possible. When an instructor changes an individual's perception, it can often be mentally confusing and difficult for the student. I used to take pride in the fact that as a student walked away from her thirty-minute lesson, she had no idea of the massive reprogramming that had just occurred.

You can see how your mental imagery is extremely important in determining your golf swing. If you visualize the golf swing in the incorrect manner, all your practice with club position and swing technique will be to little avail. The correct mental imagery of a golf swing is as essential as a proper grip.

It Don't Mean a Thing . . .

Don't expect your golf swing to change in a moment. Accept change as both a process and a discipline. Try first to understand the general motion of a golf swing and remember that the swing is a motion that incorporates different positions, not a series of positions that create a motion. When you take the swing out of golf, you are left with a contrived mechanical motion that is not bound by a general swinging motion—which, in essence, leaves you without a golf swing. Remember the lyrics of the Duke Ellington song: "It don't mean a thing if you ain't got that swing!"

PART III

Practice for Power

14

Power Drills

This chapter presents a number of drills for you to achieve maximum power in golf. Some have been referenced earlier in the book and are specifically designed to work with certain techniques. Practice them regularly and you will see results.

Swinging-arms drill and torso rotation: This is one of the best drills for teaching both a proper shoulder turn and the general swing motion. Assume your regular address position. Place your feet together. Raise the club to the top of your backswing and swing through to your finish. Once you reach your finish, swing the club back to its backswing position. This should be a continuous swinging motion. However, be sure that your feet remain planted on the ground and use as little lower-body motion as possible. Repeat this exercise about twenty times, simply swinging back and forth.

This exercise is great for displaying how the power center moves through the swing. Since the power center cannot move without the shoulders turning, this exercise reinforces the proper shoulder rotation and gives you a good feel of the swinging motion. After you do this exercise about twenty times, you will be as loose as a goose. And in such a state your arms will swing freely. The fact that you swing through to your finish and then allow the club to swing back to its backswing position is great for getting a feel for how fast the arms should swing on the backswing. The momentum from swinging backward from your finish to the top of the backswing gives the arms speed and promotes a faster wrist cock.

A variation on this exercise involves actually hitting golf balls. When performing this exercise, place the ball on a tee until you get confident enough to hit it off the ground. Assume your normal address position, with your feet positioned a shoulder's length apart. Now step backward about 4 feet. Start your back-and-forth swinging motion very smoothly and not too quickly. Now approach the ball very slowly while continuing to swing. Continue swinging until you are finally so close to the ball that it can be hit on your downswing. Do not change your tempo or speed; simply let your arms swing and watch the ball fly. It will amaze you how little effort it takes to produce such a powerful shot.

Warning: When you perform this drill, make sure that no one is standing directly to your right. I have seen golfers perform this exercise and accidentally hit the ball while swinging to the top of their backswing position. Although the ball is hit with the back of the club, it can travel quite fast and hit an innocent bystander pretty hard.

The hip-rotation drill: This drill requires a ball the size of a basketball. Assume your normal stance. Put the ball between your legs, holding it in position by squeezing with your knees. Now swing your club back and through. This exercise teaches proper hip rotation on the backswing and follow-through. Your hips have to be restricted in their movement in order for your knees and thighs to keep the ball in place. This restriction will also promote greater upper-body rotation.

Segmentation drill: This drill is designed for the better understanding of segmentation (see chapter 3). In this drill we will use a putter. First, grip your putter, and instead of assuming your normal stance, try to bend as little as possible. Your arms should be in a straight line with your wrists. Your back and legs should be as straight as possible (but only so straight that you are still able to reach the ground). When you take the club back, notice how your body seems to function as a unit. Now bend at your hips and make your backstroke. See how your lower body's movement is less affected by the upper body's (and vice versa)? Now bend at your forearms. See how your forearm and hand movement are less affected by your shoulders? This is the segmentation theory. You should bend at every part of your body to discover how that particular bend or segmentation affects your general motion. When you understand segmentation, you will better understand the effect of your body's position on the golf swing.

Hands-through-impact drill: The purpose of these drills is to educate the hands as to their proper role on the downswing. By educating the hands, I mean training them in their correct positions during the swing. (I strongly suggest rereading the hand's release section in chapter 2 before performing these drills.) We will train each hand individually, then together.

The right hand: Put your left hand on your power center and grip the club with your right. Swing the club back until the toe of the club points toward the sky. Allow your power center to turn about 40 degrees toward the right. Now allow the arm, hand, and club head to move back toward the ball. As the club face begins to point toward the ball, your power center will do the same. Once the club face is directly behind the ball, it will be pointing toward your target. As your shoulders and power center begin to point toward the target, the toe of the club will again point toward the sky. All the time this is happening, the hand should move in straight alignment with the club head (see Figs. 47, 48, and 49). Do not let the hands swing the club head.

FIGURE 47. The wrist is cocked.

FIGURE 48. The wrist has straightened.

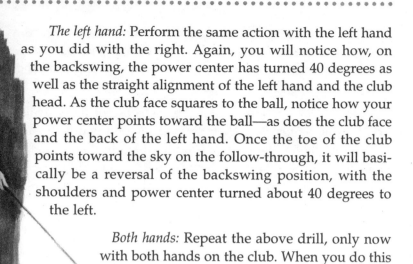

FIGURE 49. On the follow-through, allow the toe of the club to point toward the sky.

The left hand: Perform the same action with the left hand as you did with the right. Again, you will notice how, on the backswing, the power center has turned 40 degrees as well as the straight alignment of the left hand and the club head. As the club face squares to the ball, notice how your power center points toward the ball—as does the club face and the back of the left hand. Once the toe of the club points toward the sky on the follow-through, it will basically be a reversal of the backswing position, with the shoulders and power center turned about 40 degrees to the left.

Both hands: Repeat the above drill, only now with both hands on the club. When you do this exercise, the wrists should not break; rather, they should move as they did with only one hand. Now place a ball on a tee and execute this motion. Realize that at the most the ball will travel only a few feet, so do not try to hit at the ball. After the ball is struck, look at your finish. Make sure that the right wrist is not pronated and that the left wrist is not supinated. Your first and most natural inclination will be to force the club head at the ball, so remember to keep the hands moving in a straight line with the club face.

Now swing the club so that the hands reach hip level and let them swing back and forth in this same manner. This is the hand release. The only difference between this and a full swing is that the hands will be moving at a greater velocity so that the wrists will swivel more.

Hand-release drill: Most release drills emphasize the flipping of the hands at impact. We want to do the opposite. We will not practice a flipping motion; rather, we will combine a straightening and a torque motion with the wrists. It is important to do this exercise in slow motion. Grip the club with your right hand only. Now swing the club back to hip level, allowing the wrist to cock about 60 degrees. Swing the club back toward the ball and keep the wrist cocked until the palm of the right hand points toward the ball. At this point allow your wrist to uncock (straighten 45 degrees; see Figs. 47 and 48). Immediately after the wrist uncocks, allow the toe of the club to point toward the sky (Fig. 49). The motion you have just executed is what is commonly called the wrist release.

Right-elbow drill: This exercise will demonstrate how the

right elbow does not move intentionally into the right side on the downswing. First, put your left hand on the club's head. Now place your right hand on the center of the shaft. Swing the club back and allow your right elbow to bend (as in a full swing). On the downswing, let the club come back in front of you. You will probably notice that the right elbow moves in toward the right hipbone and that this occurred with no intentional effort on your part.

The "stay connected" drill: In chapter 6, we discussed how the hand release followed the power center's movement. This drill is designed to help you better understand this concept.

This is a rather unusual drill and one that will require you to assume an awkward position. When performing this drill, bear in mind that everyone has a different build and level of flexibility. If at any point you feel uncomfortable, elevate your body to a less stressful position. I would strongly urge that anyone who has back problems skip this drill. If you get the gist of the drill, you should be able to understand the idea I am trying to convey without actually performing the drill.

Often when explaining a complex movement it is best to start at the core movement and expand. In this exercise, we will begin with the closest distance possible between the hands and the club head and then gradually increase our distance, or spatial relationship. Take a nine-iron and assume your normal grip. Now bend and grip the metal shaft of the club about 8 inches from the club head. Be careful not to bend to the point that the position is uncomfortable or that you might hurt your back. The butt of the club should point toward and touch (if physically possible) the center of your stomach. Now swing the club back so that the toe of the club points toward the sky. Swing down your target line until the toe of the club points toward the sky. During this entire motion the butt of the club should be touching the center of your stomach. Notice the relationship between your power center, hands, club shaft, and club face. They are all moving at the same relative speed. Now gradually grip a little higher on the shaft and swing back and through. As you begin to grip higher and higher, allow the butt of the club to slowly move away from, but still let it point toward, your stomach. As the power center turns, the arms and hands move. The hands have a greater distance to travel than the power center, so the higher your grip on the club (more toward the butt of the club), the faster your hands will move to stay in sync with the center's movement.

Now let's do this same exercise with a minor adjustment. This time, grip the club 8 inches from the club head. Now swing the club back and allow your wrists to slightly cock so that the club's shaft is parallel or even pointing slightly toward the sky. When swinging back through again, be sure the butt of the club points toward or touches the center of your stomach as it did at the address. Then allow the club to swing so that the toe of the club points toward the sky and the butt toward the center of your stomach on the follow-through. Continue to grip higher, and as you do so, take more of a backswing until you reach your full backswing with the 90-degree wrist cock. When you swing at this point, the club's butt will not touch your stomach but will still point in the same general direction. Also, do this exercise in slow motion. This is an exercise purely for the understanding of the relative motion between the club, the hands, and the power center.

The Y drill: The Y drill is also designed to teach the proper relationship between the power center, the hands, and the club head. At the address, form the letter Y (your arms are the Y's top and the club's shaft is the Y's stem). Swing the club toward the right so that the stem of the Y is parallel to the ground and the Y's top points toward the sky. Now allow the Y to swing through to a similar position on the follow-through. Once again, the stem of the Y will be parallel to the ground, while the Y's top will point toward the sky. By moving the Y in this manner you have forced the power center, the hands, and club head to rehearse the correct motion through impact.

Let's take it one step further. This time, on your backswing and your follow-through allow the stem of the Y to point toward the sky. This means that the wrists are cocking on the backswing and follow-through. When the hands swing, this Y will stay together through impact. Now simply allow the cocked stem of the Y to reach the top of the backswing and follow-through. This is your full swing. Practice this several times, beginning with the little Y and increasing to the full swing. This will give you the correct idea of how the swing should stay connected through impact.

Wrist-cocking drill: If your wrists are slow to cock on the backswing, this drill will help. When you address the ball, instead of your arms and the club's shaft forming the letter Y, allow the hands to be positioned behind the ball (more toward your right foot). When the hands are positioned as such, they must work twice as hard to get the club head into position. This exercise should be used at the practice range with the objective of teaching the wrists to be more active on the backswing.

Power-assembly drill: Swing the club to the top of the backswing. Now swing down until your hands are at about hip level. Make sure your left arm is perfectly straight and your wrists are still cocked. In an effort to maintain that position, you should feel tension in the left and right arms and hands. Keep that position for about twenty seconds without relaxing the arms or your grip pressure. Once in this position, alternate your focus. First look at the ball, then look at the power assembly. Try to keep both the ball and the assembly in view as much as possible. This drill will reinforce your muscle memory of the correct movement of the power assembly on the downswing.

15

Golf Exercises

This chapter contains two types of exercises: those that will increase your body strength while you rehearse the proper golf-swing motion and those that are designed to increase the strength of swing-related muscles.

Although a powerful swing is one that incorporates technique, general fitness and physical strength are still necessary for distance. You have to remember that the golf swing is an athletic motion; your body should be in good enough condition to react to the athletic motion that it is about to perform. Also, if one area of your body is unusually weak, you will want to target that area for exercise. Although it may not be vital to the execution of a good swing, your body must react to the swinging motion, and when one area falls behind, another area will have to compensate. For example, the golfer who has strong legs and weak forearms will have to fight the tendency for her legs to dominate. Any increase in arm strength will be a plus.

Many women will see an increase in distance just by improving their forearm and hand strength. If you couple this increase in strength with improvement in your swing's technique, you should see at least an additional 10 yards off the tee. I think that you will find, if you practice these exercises religiously and work on your swing's fundamentals, that you will soon be hitting the ball farther than you thought you could. So let us now take a look at some of the exercises that will put you on the path to a power swing.

Practice Between Shots

Many golfers complain about not having enough time in which to practice their swings. In today's world, where many women juggle their roles as both mother and breadwinner, this is quite understandable. Everyone needs time off, and golf is a great break from a hectic schedule. The only problem is that without practice it is difficult to play at an enjoyable level on the golf course. The solution is to practice on the course. I am not advocating going onto the course by yourself and hitting three or four balls per hole. Golf should be played on the golf course; that means hitting one ball and *counting all your strokes!* Going out and hitting three or four balls does not help your swing. It may help you with course management by allowing you to get a feel for different distances and angles of playing each hole, but as for helping your swing, it lulls you into a sense of false security because you know that you can always drop another ball.

Practice between shots. For the player to have enough time to practice on a driving range is just that much more of a bonus! The time spent between shots varies with the speed of play. On most golf courses during peak months, there is a considerable wait on each hole. Instead of focusing on how slow the players in front of you are moving, focus on your swing. Golf is a sociable sport, so I am not advocating going off by yourself. There are exercises that can be used on the golf course while you are having a conversation, waiting for your next shot.

Be careful of two things when you do these exercises. First, make sure that no one can be hit by your club, even if it should come loose in your hand. Second, make sure your swings are in the rough or outside the tee box (in case of any accidental divots). Always test the parameters of the exercise you are about to perform. For example, if you are practicing a technique that requires an arm's length of distance, fully extend your arms to see what this encompasses, and whom it might affect.

The first exercise will enable you to learn to grip the club correctly, and it will also strengthen your hand. Place your left hand on the club. Be sure that the heel of your left hand is on top of the club's shaft (see Fig. 50A). If the heel of the left hand has been placed correctly, you will feel your forearm straighten as your hand grips the club. Assume your normal setup procedure, only this time, leave the right hand off the club. Now, with the last two fingers of the left hand, squeeze tightly, then release. As you do this, the club

FIGURE 50A. The heel of the left hand on top of the club.

FIGURE 50B. When you apply pressure with the last two fingers and the heel of the left hand, the wrists will naturally cock.

should rise and fall (see Fig. 50B). These are the pressure points that should be applied by the left hand. When doing this exercise, make sure that the left arm is straight. Do not allow the elbow to bend. Do this exercise anytime you are standing or sitting with the club in your hand. It will strengthen your forearm, and when it is time to grip the club, you will naturally apply pressure correctly with these fingers.

If you stop and think about it, the little finger of your left hand is not the strongest part of your body, so any increase in strength will be beneficial! One trick to increase strength is to hold a golf ball in your left hand, squeeze, and then release with the last two fingers. Repeat this motion as often as possible. Isometrics are a great way to increase strength, and something as simple as squeezing a golf ball can be done while you are riding in the cart.

Now, with the right hand, assume your normal grip (club in the fingers). Remove your thumb and little finger. Swing to the top of your backswing holding the club with just these fingers. Swing through to your finish. It is important to strengthen these fingers. It is equally important to train the right hand in its role during the swing. Assuming that you are right-handed, the right arm will try to dominate on the downswing. It is this desire to dominate that creates a casting motion in nine out of ten cases. Therefore, it is imperative to train the right arm to be submissive. While practicing this submissive behavior, we want to encourage the proper pressure points which will hopefully deter the tendency to cast. The trick in this exercise is that at the top of your swing your fingers should be perched talonlike (see Fig. 51). If the right hand is perched too upright, the club will drop out of your fingers. However, if the pads of the right hand and fingers are correctly positioned to support the club, you will find that it will require very little pressure to place the club into position at the top of your swing.

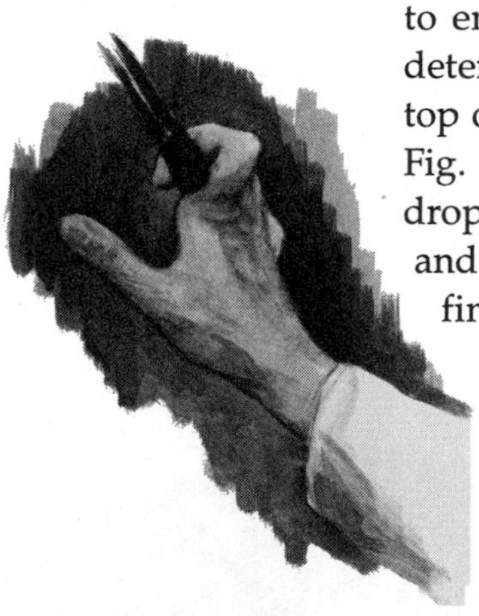

Hold the club with a straight left arm so that the shaft of the club and your arm are parallel with the ground. Now cock your left wrist so that the shaft of the club is pointing toward the sky, perpendicular to the ground. Repeat this twenty times. Be sure that you keep your left arm straight and that the club starts from its parallel position. Also, make sure you hang on with the last three fingers of the left hand. Do not cheat by cocking with the fingers rather than the wrists. While doing this, accent the upward movement of the wrist cock, not the downward movement (a casting motion). This

FIGURE 51. The shaft of the club is nestled into the fingers of the right hand, with the index finger forming a talon.

is a great exercise to increase strength in your left arm and wrist; it will also teach you the correct cocking motion of the wrists. After completing the twenty repetitions, let your arm hang and shake it for several minutes to relax the muscles. After you feel secure in your ability to do twenty repetitions, increase the drill in increments of five. It will be difficult at first, but hang in there. Building these muscles is as important as hitting buckets of balls. This exercise can be done while you are waiting to hit your next shot. Just make sure when doing this exercise that your shadow cannot be seen by any golfer preparing to hit their shot. The shadow of a club being repetitively lifted into the air can be a little distracting while making a putt!

Another great exercise is to grip the club with your left hand and swing it to the top of your backswing. Make sure your left arm is straight, with the wrists cocked 90 degrees. Let your arm return about 15 inches on the same plane as your backswing, then raise it to the top of the backswing. At first, do this as often as you can. On the last repetition let the club swing through to its finish. You should have built up enough tension that this should come as a relief. Be sure that the left arm is perfectly straight. This straightness is necessary to build the correct muscles. This is also a very difficult exercise, so take your time, increase repetitions in small increments, and be sure to let your arm fall limp afterward, shaking it to relax the muscles. This exercise can be performed while you are talking to your partners as well as when you are waiting to tee off.

This exercise does not reinforce any swing motion. It will simply strengthen targeted muscles in your arm. With your left arm parallel to the ground, hold the club in your left hand with the wrist fully cocked. This will leave the club at a right angle to the left arm and pointing toward the sky. Now turn your wrist to the right so that the club is parallel to the ground and the back of the left hand is pointing toward the sky. Now turn to its previous position. Next, turn the hand to the left so that the palm of the left hand is pointing toward the sky and the club is parallel to the ground. Then turn back to the club's original position. Do this as many times as you can.

The next time, swing the club back with just the right hand. At the top of your backswing, notice the position of your power assembly. Try to keep the power assembly in this position as you swing back toward the ground. Don't allow your assembly to straighten until the palm of your right hand begins to point down your target line. This exercise is great to practice while you are waiting for your next shot. When executed correctly, it will train the power assembly to stay together, plus reinforce the proper downswing plane.

Last but not least is the standard left-arm drill. Touring professionals use this one between shots. Simply swing the club with only your left arm. Swinging with the left arm reinforces proper shoulder rotation and forces you to delay the release (uncocking) of the wrist. This all happens naturally when swinging with the left arm. This drill will also increase the muscle strength of the left arm, which is a tremendous benefit for most right-handed players.

While these exercises will help your swing, a simple increase in muscle tone or strength often can increase the distance of your tee shots. Most women would benefit from an increase in strength in their hands, wrists, arms, and forearms. Also, women with narrow shoulders or weak shoulder muscles will benefit from exercises that target the shoulder area. Any exercise that increases the strength in any of these muscles will be helpful in creating a powerful swing. If you lift weights, lightweight repetitions targeting the forearms, wrists, hands, and shoulders are the most beneficial to your golf swing. Stretching exercises are also important. When your muscles are tight, your body cannot operate at optimum performance. So although a powerful swing is based on technique, the more you can enhance your physical strength, the better your chances for longer tee shots.

Conclusion

The greater your knowledge of the correct swing fundamentals, the greater your chances for both improving your golf game and increasing your distance. Think of your mind as a computer. When incorrect data are fed in, there is no hope for correct output. However, with the correct data input, even the simplest of programs can yield an abundance of information. Without proper mental input, there is little chance for the correct physical output on the golf swing. Throughout this book, I have given you the information necessary for a proper concept of the golf swing. I have also explained the pitfalls of certain misconceptions regarding your swing's power sources and their dramatic effect on your distance.

In the introduction I asked you to forget any preconceived limitations you might have in respect to your capabilities and to try to absorb all of the book's information as freely as possible. I hope that you not only understand that power equals technique but that because of this equation, any woman can obtain a more powerful game. My concern is not only for this physical realization but also for mental empowerment. When you step onto the golf course, I hope that you now view yourself not as a golfer destined to a monotonous routine of equally distant shots but as unfulfilled potential—a golfer who is excited and eager to awaken her capabilities.

Unfortunately, sometimes in order to keep this positive frame of mind it is necessary to wear mental blinders to keep you from being distracted by misinformed or undermining comments you may hear. Remember, women are natural golfers and very capable of hitting a powerful shot.

Throughout this book I have discussed different power sources. However, the best power source is the better understanding of the golf swing. I hope this book has started you on your journey of golf knowledge. It is my most sincere wish that it has served the purpose of laying a solid foundation for the understanding and execution of the golf swing as well as the realization that anyone is capable of improving her golf game. It is precisely because of this fact that we all—strong, weak, small, big, athletic, nonathletic—are attracted to golf. It is the equanimity of the game, the hope for improvement that we know is within our reach, that is our enjoyment. If you revel in the enjoyment of improving, I will assure you that power golf is close at hand.

This book has been directed toward women because traditionally we have been the least empowered in golf. You must realize that this lack of empowerment is a mind-set that is not realistically rooted in our capabilities. Let's put on our mental blinders, overcome this mind-set, and go play 18 holes. And when you hit a drive that travels farther than any before, don't ask yourself, Where did that come from? Rather, say to yourself with confidence, I knew I had it in me all along!

Happy golfing!

Index